D0524824

"*Postcards from the Middle East* is inspiring, challenging, and valuable. It's not easy to pigeon-hole as it's autobiography combined with a hugely helpful and well-told narrative about the politics, ecology, cultures, and religions of the region at the crossroads of the world. If you're puzzled by what's on the news concerning Iraq, Syria, Israel, Palestine, Lebanon, and the rest of the Middle East, this is a great place to start. It's told with humour and empathy, and most of all with deep love for the people and the places where many of today's global tensions focus. Read it soon and you'll not only be better informed, you'll see the people and region quite differently."
Reverend Dave Bookless, Director of Theology, A Rocha International

"This is Christianity bringing real hope to the wildlife, wild places, and the people of Lebanon's Bekaa Valley and beyond. It is an extraordinary tale of faith in action with cultural and historical insights sandwiched in regional turmoil."
David Chandler, co-author of *RSPB Guide to Birdwatching*

"This is a very readable and compelling account of a family living through tumultuous events in the Middle East. I can't think of a better way of getting beneath the surface and understanding something of the culture, religion, and politics of the region than through the very varied experiences of Chris and Susanna and their family. Having lived through some of these same events and seen their creative conservation work in Lebanon, I can vouch for the fact that it made a very significant contribution in a troubled country."
Reverend Colin Chapman, formerly lecturer in Islamic Studies, Near East School of Theology, Beirut, Lebanon

"The environmental condition of the Middle East is easily forgotten amidst the maelstrom of politics and conflict. This rich and inspiring account of the Naylor family's adventures in Lebanon, and the setting up of A Rocha's project to help protect the priceless Aammiq wetlands in the Bekaa Valley, will help put many a conservation battle into perspective. It is thoughtful, wise, and compelling reading, with enough name-dropping of exciting fauna to make you thirst to go there yourself."
Dominic Couzens, bestselling natural history writer and author of *Secret Lives of Garden Birds*

"More than the story of a remarkable and pioneering family and the conservation organization they led, *Postcards from the Middle East* gives a hard-won and deeply grounded perspective on a beautiful and troubled country whose history has come to affect us all. Chris Naylor's knowledgeable affection for the landscapes and cultures he gave so much to understand, and for the Lebanese people whose current diaspora are found all around the world, shines through every page. With every chapter, we become the beneficiaries of his many years in the region; the extraordinary legacy of his working years there give him a wise and moderate voice that deserves to be widely heard."
Peter Harris, President and co-founder of A Rocha

"Chris Naylor has reminded me of a carpet weaver in Medhat Bacha market in old Damascus. He was able to skilfully weave in various threads of culture, family, history, religion, mythology, and politics to produce a colourful carpet. Naylor's lucid and conversational style makes the book an enjoyable reading. I appreciated his cultural sensitivity and authentic sincerity as he shares his and his family's experiences and adventures. This book deserves to be placed next to Edward Said's *Orientalism*, but I assure you that you will read it with lots of smiles and laughter!"
Dr Riad Kassis, Director, Langham Scholars Ministry, Langham Partnership

"Weaving together colourful anecdotes and astute observations, Chris Naylor explores themes of faith, community, and nature conservation in the beautifully written and evocative story of one British family's life in Kuwait, Jordan, and Lebanon. This warm-hearted and honest book is a must-read for anyone who wants to better understand the cultural, political, and religious complexities of the Middle East."

Dr Hilary Marlow, Faraday Institute for Science and Religion

"This well written book is an inspiring story of life in the Middle East with many interesting details about the people, the natural history, and the religions of the region."

Professor Sir Ghillean Prance, FRS, Former Director, Royal Botanic Gardens, Kew

"Like the best tapestry, this book has so many beautiful elements weaving through it. It is a colourful description of an amazing time spent in the Middle East, blended wonderfully with an exploration of the history and culture of that significant part of the world. His love for, and care of, the people who live there, the land they live on, and the other creatures they share that land with, shines through in everything he writes. As the troubles in that part of the world just keep escalating, this is a book we all should read."

Dr Ruth Valerio, author of *L is for Lifestyle: Christian living that doesn't cost the earth*

Postcards from the Middle East

CHRIS NAYLOR

LION

For Susanna, Sam, Chloe, and Josh

Published by Lion Books
an imprint of
Lion Hudson plc
Wilkinson House, Jordan Hill Road,
Oxford OX2 8DR, England
www.lionhudson.com/lion

ISBN 978 0 7459 5649 7
e-ISBN 978 0 7459 5650 3

First edition 2015

Acknowledgments
Scripture quotations marked NIV are taken from the Holy Bible, New International Version Anglicised. Copyright © 1979, 1984, 2011 Biblica, formerly International Bible Society. Used by permission of Hodder & Stoughton Ltd, an Hachette UK company. All rights reserved. "NIV" is a registered trademark of Biblica. UK trademark number 1448790.

Scripture quotations marked NLT are taken from the Holy Bible, New Living Translation, copyright © 1996, 2004, 2007 by Tyndale House Foundation. Used by permission of Tyndale House Publishers, Inc., Carol Stream, Illinois 60188. All rights reserved.

Extract p. 85 taken from *Lawrence of Arabia*. Courtesy of Columbia Pictures.

p. 8 Map of Lebanon © Samuel Naylor.

Plate section: photographs of the White Stork, Short-toed Eagle, and the Honey Buzzard © Peter Harris

A catalogue record for this book is available from the British Library

Printed and bound in the UK, February 2015, LH26

Contents

Map of Lebanon

Acknowledgments

This book covers a period of two decades and so implicates many family and friends. My greatest thanks go to my wife Susanna and children Samuel, Chloe, and Joshua for allowing our family story to be told and for their advice, recollections and arguments that helped shape the book. I am also grateful to Barbara Mearns, George and Mary Kopti, Tom Rowley, Stephen and Marianne Raikes, Colin Chapman, Michel Skaff, Richard Storey, Chris Walley, Peter Harris, Andy and Laurel Sprenger, Joy Mallouh, Colin Conroy and Jennie Evans who read either parts or all of the text to check that my memories weren't too far from the truth.

The fact that our family musings have progressed to a book is thanks to Lion Hudson, and particularly to Tony Collins for believing in the project and to my commissioning editor Ali Hull for the Herculean task of sharpening the text and straightening out my idiosyncratic grammar.

My greatest thanks go to the people of Lebanon for taking us into their hearts and changing us for good.

A Note on Transliteration of Arabic to English Text

Recording Arabic words in Roman script is fraught with challenges, the greatest of which is consistency. Let me give you an example. The region of Aammiq that looms large in the central chapters of the book is variously recorded on maps, road signs, reports and in literature as Aammiq, Ammiq, Amiq, Amik, Ameek and even 9amiq!

In an attempt to remain consistent and give the reader a chance to sound out the words I have attempted to stick to two simple rules:

1. The transliteration is phonetic but does not make use of special symbols for sounds which have no English equivalent. Thus the Islamic holy text is written "Qur'an" not "Ḳur'ān".

2. Where Arabic names have wide use in English I opt for the English form that is in most common use, even if it is not the best transliteration – e.g. Bekaa Valley.

A note on names

The stories and incidents in the book have been recorded as accurately as my memory allowed. However, a few of the names of people and places have been changed to maintain anonymity where that is important.

To Picnic or Not to Picnic?

Summer, 1995
Aammiq wetland, the Bekaa Valley, Lebanon

It was time to explore. We had arrived in the Bekaa valley a month ago but, without a car, had only got to know the village and a taste of the surrounding countryside. The panorama of fertile plain abruptly interrupted by the towering, dusty heights of the Anti-Lebanon hills, with Mount Hermon brooding to the south, invited us further in.

Now we had a car. And we were off.

This was not our first Arab country. Susanna and I had lived in Kuwait immediately (and I mean immediately) before the first Gulf War. After that year, and a time of putting our lives together in the UK after the war, we had returned to the region – first living the highs and lows, joys and pain of learning Arabic in Jordan. Now we were in the Lebanon. This was not going to be a short adventure, either – we were intending to stay. But all that was on our minds that particular morning was getting the kids in the car, packing a picnic and heading into the scenery that had so tantalized us from our balcony eyrie perched at the top of the town of Qab Elias.

We headed south. Leaving the narrow, congested streets, swerving round the donkey grazing on the rubbish spilling out of the dry riverbed, we left the dust, the noise and the colour of our adopted neighbourhood, and drove into the cool green of the irrigated fields that made up the West Bekaa. Neighbours, fast becoming friends, had told us of a local picnic spot that was safe. Abu Ali had been very insistent on where we should go. He had patiently listened to our plans for exploring, our desire to head into the foothills of the mountains to the east, to find tracks to follow into the woods on the plain, or perhaps even reach the top of the Barouk ridge to the west. He simply said, "No! *Gayr amena!*" It is not safe!

Mines and unexploded ordnance still littered the countryside. The chessboard fields had played host to local militias and invading armies over the past three decades. The front line stand-off between the Israelis and Syrians in the 1980s was just a few miles to the south of the town. We had provisionally earmarked some of the most likely spots from poring over our local map, but riverbanks or ridges with the promise of panoramic views produced dire warnings of maimings from Abu Ali: "Don't you love your children? Why would you take them to such a place?" Eventually our probing questions elicited the directions to a local beauty spot that was considered safe – if we felt we had to explore, even though it was far too hot and there really wasn't much to see, and we must be careful of the snakes... and we were off.

It was clear by the number of cars parked on the verge by the roadside that many of our fellow villagers did not share Abu Ali's pessimism but were enjoying family and food by the delphinium-blue pools fed from the aquifer deep under the mountain immediately behind us. Whole families had taken up residence under the few remaining trees by the water's edge. Vast tablecloths were spread with fruit, flatbread, salads, marinating meat, pastries and countless Tupperware containers cradling unknown delicacies. Women enrobed against the sun and prying eyes were flapping and strutting around the growing feasts like the Great White Egrets in the marshland beyond the pools. Men reclined in semicircles of camp chairs, taking it in turns to draw deep lungfuls of smoke from the *nargile* pipes topped with glowing tobacco.

Running between the culinary islands the children laughed, played and fought, a riot of noise and energy disturbing the practised aim of the young men who were trying to shoot water snakes, as they criss-crossed the pools in search of small fish. Occasional retorts pinpointed the more serious hunters deep in the wetland reed beds, away from the disturbance of their kin, after the larger game of herons, storks or, if they were really lucky, a buzzard or eagle to stuff and mount as a trophy back home.

We stood motionless, appalled, by the car. What were we going to do?

Our own children impatiently tugged on our arms, urging us on to join the party. They wanted to play in the water. It was too hot to stand by the road.

"Let's go down there!" said four-year-old Sam, pointing to the drama unfolding by the pool.

It was not the image we had longed for during the month we had been stuck in the noisy, busy, crowded town. Here we were, finally in the "countryside" but the town had beaten us to it! Susanna and I had arrived, complete with our British expectations of what a picnic spot should be, and we were sorely disappointed. But we had not come to Lebanon for picnics, we had come to get to know and understand the local people, the Lebanese, the Arabs and from that understanding share our faith. A faith first lived out just on the other side of the mountain overlooking this beautiful but noisy marsh. And so we joined the picnic.

To the pulsating drumbeat of the Derbakeh – the classic Lebanese hand-held drum – we made our way through the shaded feasts laid out on the grass, entreated by family after family: "*Mayilu! Mayilu!* Join us! Join us!"

Choosing a vacant spot near one of the more insistent families, we settled down to unpack our embarrassingly small picnic. It didn't matter. We were soon proffered succulent chicken, perfectly cooked on recycled tin barbeques, steaming and wrapped in flatbread. Our plates were piled high with *tabbouleh* and *fattoush* salads, *kibbe* meatballs with fresh goats' milk yoghurt, stuffed vine leaves and *homous*, as the al fresco mezze went on and on. The children were soon the centre of attention of a crowd of adoring adults and Susanna was being quizzed, principally on whom we were related to in the valley. Questions were fired from several directions at once:

"You are the foreigners living in *Bayt Kassis*, the apartment above the Evangelical School, aren't you?"

"Is it true you have come from London? It is always foggy in London, isn't it?"

"Who are your family in Lebanon?"

"Do you really not have any family in the country? But how awful!"

"What is your family name? Naylor – but that's a girl's name – you can't be called Naylor!"

At this point a rather shy teenager was pushed to the front, her hijab pulled tightly round her lower face to conceal braces, the mark of teenagers the world over. "This is Nayla!"

Our local identity could never be in our extended family, but in common with all parents in the valley we were known in relation to our children – or to be more precise, with reference to our son; so we became Um and Abu Sami (mother and father of Sam). Our two-year-old daughter, Chloe, didn't get a look-in.

"Really? No Lebanese family? How dreadful to be on your own…" I drifted off in the direction of the lads who were trying to kill the snakes.

"Do you want a go?" asked the nearest marksman.

"No, thanks. I like snakes and I don't want to kill a harmless creature that is not doing me any harm," I replied.

"He sounds like Yusef!" called a tall, immaculately dressed boy, as he threw his Coke bottle into the nearby pool. "He likes snakes; he likes all sorts of creepy animals."

I decided I needed to meet Yusef and so, after explaining that I was going to be the new science teacher at the large secondary school in the valley (which seemed to explain my weird views on animal life), I was escorted by a gaggle of boys and young men into the wetland proper, on the trail of Yusef. These lads knew the paths that criss-crossed the drier parts of the reed bed and hidden meadows that took us deeper into the marshes, away from the sound of traffic and picnickers, into a still world, muffled by the curtains of reeds, sun-bleached, dry feathery heads craning upwards to the cornflower blue of the sky.

Initially we brought our own noise with us, raucous and shrill as the entourage enjoyed the energy of the pack, sending water rails scurrying into the undergrowth. Purple Herons, breaking cover at the last minute in an explosion of wings, lifted their elongated frames clear of the reeds. But soon the magic of the place took hold and a hush descended on the group. We followed paths made by wild creatures, boar and maybe hyena or swamp cats – away from the road with its apron of grass playing host to the village party – into an oasis of peace, untouched by humankind.

"Stop!" shouted Abdallah, our self-appointed leader, pointing to the lopsided fence with its lonely wire draped around the rough corner of the field, nestled on two sides by the dog-leg of a tiny river.

"*Al Gaam!* Mines!"

Not so untouched by humankind after all. As if to mark the counterpoint of realities, a sonic boom detonated overhead with a second close on its heels – Israeli jets, breaking the sound barrier on their return home. Sure enough, arcing vapour trails pinpointed the interruption as Lebanon's neighbour flexed its military muscle, just in case anyone forgot they controlled the sky. A daily event, it did little more than cause a slight pause in conversation, but the wetland erupted as great flocks of ducks and waders exploded from the hidden pools. Soon they were swirling in decreasing circles, the tiny forms of the waders coming to ground first, the ducks, harried by hunters, struggling to find a safe landing.

I was bombarded with emotion. In the glorious peace and wildness of this place, with the sun on our backs and the majesty of the eastern mountains marching their way to the Syrian Desert beyond, I had been enjoying the company of an infectiously enthusiastic band of lads in a sanctuary of rare natural beauty. A few more steps and one or more of us would have been blown up.

I was also struggling to make sense of the attitudes I had encountered among the Lebanese youth around me. They clearly loved this place – but, from my very British perspective, they diminished it with their litter, noise and random hunting. Was this typical Lebanese behaviour? Was it part of the culture, or did attitudes vary here as much as they did back home? Was there a Lebanese view on hunting, nature, noise… anything? Did the Lebanese view their surroundings like other Arabs? Was there an Arab way of looking at the world?

These questions are issues of identity, and as I write on this topic I feel that I am back in that minefield in the marsh. I am sure I will put a step wrong and I will get blown up. But it is important territory to map out. In many ways this book is an attempt to make patterns and connections from our experiences as a British family living in the Arab world, to better understand it and its people.

Talking about the Arab world is a good place to start, although the definition in Wikipedia hints of trouble to come when it states: "No universally accepted definition of 'the Arab world' exists, but it is generally assumed to include the twenty-two countries belonging to the Arab League that have a combined population of about 280 million…"[1]

Treading even more gingerly, let's try to go a step further in the minefield without dire consequences – who, then, is an Arab?

Feeling vulnerable and so seeking confidence in the academic kudos of the Oxford dictionary, we find: "a member of a Semitic people, originally from the Arabian Peninsula and neighboring territories, inhabiting much of the Middle East and North Africa."[2]

---

[1] http://en.wikipedia.org/wiki/Arab_world (accessed 3.11.14).
[2] http://oxforddictionaries.com/us/definition/american_english/Arab (accessed 3.11.14).

And so we step on a mine. Yusef, whom we eventually found in the wetland, would not have wanted to classify himself as having forebears from the Arabian Peninsula. He was proud of his Phoenician roots, but he would describe himself as an Arab. Several of his family members liked to draw the distinction between their Phoenician identity and the Arabs who came from Syria with their flocks, much as Bedouin wanderers have for millennia. And let's not get started with religion. It is a common misconception in the West that Arabs are Muslim. Six million Coptic Christians in Egypt and the very constitution of the state of Lebanon dismantle that simplification.

Perhaps language will help – for many outsiders it is the litmus test of defining an Arab, but many of our new friends and neighbours were multilingual. The huge Arab diaspora has meant that many from an "Arab background" are more comfortable in French, English or, in the case of the Lebanese, Brazilian Portuguese, than they are in Arabic.

So what of my hope of writing about a Lebanese or an Arab perspective? There is no more an "Arab way of being" than there is a "European way of being". Italians and Danes may both be European but culturally they are very different. Although we lived in the region for a long time, we only lived in the particular Arab communities described in this book and so can only offer insights into their specific Arab stories. Nevertheless I hope, by following our journey, you will see through our slowly opening eyes something of the wealth of the culture and the depths of the struggles that are part of the tapestry of the Arab world.

Had we only known it, that picnic, in the first few weeks of our lives in the Bekaa, was a foretaste of so much to come. During our years spent in the Arab world, living, working, laughing and crying with neighbours and colleagues, many of whom became friends, we started to see things from a new perspective. We remained very firmly British (at least I did; Susanna, a third culture kid herself, never was very British and the children are a completely different story), but we started to feel, to respond, as our Arab friends did. It happened erratically and was often frustrating and awkward. We frequently got angry and were, sometimes, very difficult neighbours to be with as we got it wrong, as we misunderstood, yet again. But slowly our perspectives changed and, as they did so, we started to see why our Arab neighbours did things that way, thought the way they did, valued the things they valued. As we lived embedded within an Arab context, the things we initially saw as foreign, "other", or even wrong, started, firstly, to make sense and soon were thoroughly normal.

So many themes were wrapped up with the *khubz*, the Arabic bread, with its delicious chicken at the picnic. We had encountered extraordinary hospitality, and hospitality with joy. There was clearly an obligation to share the food, particularly with the foreigners who didn't bring enough to eat, but there was also an infectious curiosity in one another that came with that sharing. There was an extended family cohesion that was a delight to see and become a part of as our very young children were accepted and immediately valued – just for being children. There were also strong views that were very directly communicated.

Susanna should not have dressed Samuel in such a light shirt; he was too young not to have a sweater (even though it was 30 degrees C in the shade)! What was she thinking?

Several things struck us about this exchange, as we debriefed on our conversations in the car on the way home. Firstly it was only directed at Susanna – clearly, as the man I would have nothing to do with dressing the children. Secondly, the children of the mothers who said this had long since discarded their own sweaters. But perhaps, most forcibly, everything we were told was said with such complete conviction. We soon learned to listen carefully to what was being said but to basically ignore the strength of the conviction behind the words, as whenever anyone told us anything it was said as if it had just been dictated by the Almighty himself.

And what about the human disturbance of the wildlife sanctuary of the marshes, the killing of the reptiles, the shooting of the storks, and the near-ubiquitous hunting? That is a theme I will return to in earnest, but it needs a chapter of its own.

CHAPTER 1

The Middle East and
Back Again

1989–90
Kuwait and Iraq

Newly married, we nervously looked round the airport departure lounge for other likely teachers. Sure enough, it didn't take us long to spot and confirm others waiting to board the flight who had signed up to teach at one of the many international schools in Kuwait. It was immediately reassuring, after the briefest exchange of stories, to connect with other young couples, very much like us, heading off into the foreign and unfamiliar. The reasons were common currency: for adventure, to leave behind the mounting classroom bureaucracy, to experience a new culture and, of course, to earn a tax-free salary. In our case, we had an added dimension, and that was to trial a life abroad to see if we, and particularly I, were cut out for it long-term.

Susanna had grown up a child of missionaries – in Ghana, Mexico and the United States; living in England was her challenge. My upbringing had been very different. I had spent my first nineteen years in Kent, followed by university and teacher training. I had no experience of living cross-culturally. We had talked to many expatriates and they told a common story of a sense of dislocation as they learned to adapt to life in a new country. Until they adjusted, they lived with the default settings and expectations of their home culture which were constantly challenged by a very different set of norms.

But that was our plan – in "Christian speak", we felt a calling to long-term cross-cultural service, to work as Christians where the church needed us most. We hadn't really planned to do that in Kuwait – although we were open to exploring possibilities – but we were very deliberately setting out to see if we could make a life abroad as a first step to exploring how and where we would spend our future.

From our current perspective, it seems extraordinary that we felt the need to try out living abroad in such a cautious and experimental way. The truth is, however, that the thought of the heat, the distance from family and lack of cultural certainties were deeply troubling, and I just did not know how I would respond

The plane touched down late at night into thick fog. It was like Heathrow on a bleak November evening. On leaving the plane the reality struck us – we had walked into the steam room at a sauna. Relief came in the form of the air-conditioned, sparkling terminal building. The self-identified group of teachers were corralled through the immigration desks – staffed by white-robed young Kuwaiti men, each sporting a near-identical and neatly trimmed moustache, their red-and-white checked headdress casually flicked over a shoulder. They seemed bored and little interested in our passports – the paperwork the school minder provided did its job and we were stamped, processed and allowed into the emirate. The fate of a string of dispirited Bangladeshis was less clear. In contrast to the indolence of our treatment, they were receiving the full force of official wrath as their papers were clearly amiss. Grateful for our nationality but tired, we filed out of the airport and watched transfixed as the glittering coastal strip slid past, smeared as it was through the condensation on the air-conditioned minibus windows. Final destination for the night, and home for the next eleven months, was a neat but basic flat in an eleven-storey apartment block, overlooking a roundabout, in crowded Kuwait City.

In the first few days and weeks of cross-cultural living, the differentness seemed profound. This is alternately exciting and unnerving. What appears, only a few short weeks later, as mundane takes on huge significance as new ways of living are explored and compared with the familiarity of home. In the earliest stages, the inevitable contrasts are nearly universally in favour of home. This was my first cross-cultural living, and comparing the neat streets of Oxford with our new, scruffy urban Gulf Arab neighbourhood confirmed the rule. In midday temperatures of 50+ degrees C, rubbish locked in cages on street corners (to stop the army of mangy feral cats scavenging) stank. The crumbling but newly built apartment blocks groaned under the relentless sun, the pavements were not so much cracked as pot-holed and litter-strewn, and the urban landscape was haphazard. But this was only half the story. Exotic scents filled the air, fine art flapped on the breeze as exquisite carpets were aired and early morning light brought colours to life in a way I had never experienced back home. It was not just the light that accentuated colour. After the flattening heat of the day, our neighbours emerged, a riot of races and nationalities: Kuwaitis for sure, but also Armenian, Bangladeshi, Circassian – right through the alphabet to Zambians. They brought into the neon of evening a promenade of humanity in all its noisy, scented, vibrant diversity.

The oil wells of the Arabian Gulf are black holes in more ways than one. Like their celestial counterparts, they have a powerful centripetal effect on the surrounding nations and further afield. All the nationalities and ethnicities of the Middle East are to be found in the oil sheikdoms: Arabs from North Africa and the Levant; Egyptians, Moroccans, Tunisians, Syrians, Palestinians and Lebanese, but also Berbers from the Atlas Mountains, Turks from Anatolia, Persians from Iran, Kurds from Northern Iraq and Syria, and Armenians scattered by the Ottomans. Bringing with them their heritage, our block of flats and neighbourhood read like a *Who's Who* of ancient religious creeds. Certainly the two great confessions of Islam, Sunni and Shia, were well represented, but there were also Sufi and Alawite and more obscure Muslim groups, such as the Ibadi, in the form of the few Omanis living nearby.

When it came to the Middle East Christian communities, you really needed to know your church history to be able to make head or tail of the competing claims to orthodoxy. Making the Reformation seem like a recent falling out, we met Assyrian Christians who looked back to the Council of Ephesus as the great parting of the ways in AD 431, or the Syriac, Coptic or Armenian Orthodox whose schism came in AD 451 with the Council of Chalcedon and its decree on the nature of Christ. But perhaps the most surprising of all were the living fossils in this ancient sea; the Mandeans of Southern Iraq and Iran, followers of John the Baptist but not of Jesus.

Our apartment block was one of the tallest in the neighbourhood and so commanded views over the pancake roofs, deserted lots and tangles of wire and road to the sea on three sides. The block only afforded views for those willing to climb onto the flat roof, however. As we soon discovered, views from the apartments, in common with many Arab buildings, were sacrificed for privacy. Windows were small and obscured, reluctant concessions bringing limited light into the concrete cocoons protecting the families within from the harshness of the sun and prying eyes.

Veiled as it was, Kuwait City's coast was its redemption from urban ugliness. We travelled daily along this ochre shoreline as we commuted the five miles or so of the main arterial highway to a more upmarket and largely residential district. Looming above the detached white stone villas rose the school, a huge white cube, gleaming in the intense sunshine.

For young British teachers, schooled in a child-centred educational philosophy, the school was a set of contradictions. Profit competed with professionalism across the timetable. Small classes of motivated students were occasionally compromised by blatant nepotism, and staff expertise varied from excellent to the barely legal. In the official literature of the school, it described itself as being modelled on the best English public schools, providing a UK-compatible education for far-flung British expats and a host of nationalities keen to buy into an educational gold standard. GCSEs and A-levels were the traded commodity and most students achieved the grades required by their aspirational parents. Just six weeks previously I had been teaching in an excellent comprehensive school in north Oxford and the academic provision at the new school did not come close. However, as a teacher, the experience was wholly enjoyable. No longer battling with attention-deficit classes, there were ranks of delightful young Indians, Arabs and Europeans who would imbibe information as the sand in the playground would devour the rare raindrops that fell in winter.

As the academic year progressed and the searing summer heat was replaced by a delightful autumn and chilly winter, occasional educational storms would sweep through the classrooms, bringing into stark relief the contradictions at the heart of the school. The most memorable was triggered by the humble school blazer. Technically part of the school uniform but never enforced, these superfluous additions to school dress drew the ire of the older students and some parents when an edict was received from the administration that within a week, they would cloak all pupil shoulders. They were on sale from the uniform shop for the price of fifty Kuwait dinars (around £100 sterling). Leading the rebellion were the (few) British and other European students who pointed out that outside air-conditioned classrooms, the temperatures were still hotter than any northern summer and the cheap nylon material was a health hazard in the Kuwaiti climate. Early boycotts enraged the school owner who had taken delivery of a huge stock and was keen to turn a fast profit through his captive customers. Along with the other senior year tutors, a new routine was added to my day – blazer check. We had to pass on the names of all those in our tutor groups who were still blazerless, while keeping a careful check on an increasing number of counterfeit blazers, pirate items cheaply copied in the souk, to the alarm of the school owner.

Attitudes to the school administration were mixed at the best of times but Blazergate revealed the cultural differences which, ironically, were one of the strengths of the school. The petitions and boycott gave a focus for the resentment that many of the European teenagers felt towards the conservative conformist culture enveloping them. The Indian and other Asians were much less concerned and saw it as both an inevitable imposition and distraction from the serious business of learning. The Arab students – expatriate and Kuwaiti – formed a continuum between these two extremes. Their position mostly depended on how much the fifty KD would hurt their family finances. Whatever the student perspective, within a few short weeks, all pupils had a blazer. Independent learning was one thing, but independent thought was not encouraged.

When not checking up on uniform, the mechanics of my teaching role was near-identical to work in England, with the huge exception of time. Small classes and frequent free periods meant that staff could often be found in the teachers' lounge drinking coffee. A few staff would be enjoying the Irish contingent's blue jokes with their snacks even while tiny A-level sets grafted unsupervised. This was all in stark contrast to the life of the primary staff – Susanna included. With classroom teachers only getting a break when there were specialist music sessions, the life of a teacher of infants was a very busy one.

Whereas my introduction to teaching abroad had been a relative holiday, Susanna really earned her money. As well as the heavier workload, she had a very difficult line manager. A veteran of Kuwait, this manager had bullied her way through many of the English schools and was in a powerful position in her own elementary kingdom. Professionally she was stale, but financially she was committed to stay in tax-free exile, despite long since having fallen out of love with her adopted country. An all-too-common combination, it made for toxic management and Susanna, as the youngest member of staff, experienced her worst excesses.

As the victimization showed no signs of abating, we took advice from more experienced staff and hatched a plan. Normal mechanisms for staff complaint were non-existent and it was clear that staff support was dished out on the basis of favouritism. We got to know the influential senior staff, and when I let it be known that we were thinking of leaving as Susanna was experiencing such harsh treatment from her line manager, the news found its way to the top. A sideways move meant that Susanna suddenly had a superb supervisor in the form of our very good friend Marianne.

We had not realized at the time but we were playing a high-stakes game, as defections by the staff and instant dismissal were common events. At the end of each holiday, there would be notable absences as certain teachers failed to return from travels overseas. They had quietly sorted out their affairs and got out of contractual obligations mid-term by simply leaving the country. The reasons behind these staff disappearances became clear whenever a teacher was in dispute with the school. The only disputes possible with the administration were appeal against immediate dismissal – the usual sanction if your face did not fit. One teacher took the school to court under the extensive Kuwaiti labour laws, only to be greeted by the judge and school owner enjoying a coffee together when he arrived early for the hearing. He was on the next plane out of the emirate.

As the academic year turned, we were frustrated with our lack of engagement with the Kuwaiti culture around us. We enjoyed friendships within the expatriate social circle of school, connected as it was to other networks. However, one of our motivations for life outside the UK was to see another culture from the inside. And that meant getting to know and share our lives with our neighbours, not just our work colleagues who were transplants like us. With no Arabic and busy working lives (at least in Susanna's case), this was harder than we thought. We did meet Kuwaiti parents, but engagement was tightly defined by professional protocols and the

Kuwaitis we knew in this context seemed intensely private and happy to keep relationships on an "upstairs downstairs" basis.

It was church that gave us the social space to meet and truly get to know a representative cross-section of the residents of the nation. Although conspicuous by their absence, the conservative Muslim Kuwaitis were a minority in their own land and the evangelical church that we attended more truly represented the ethnic melting pot that made up the workforce of the state. There were over twenty congregations that met in the downtown church compound – a relic of earlier days when medical missionaries provided the only hospital care for an impoverished nation of pearl fishers.

Our congregation, defined by English, was one of the big four, and here we got to know fellow believers from ancient churches in Goa, Mesopotamia, Armenia, Egypt, Lebanon, Syria and Palestine, as well as those from the Philippines, Europe, North and South America.

So many of our new friends had extraordinary stories. We became friends with three sisters from Bethlehem, without passports, born in Kuwait, the eldest studying to be a doctor but with no right of travel outside the cubic borders of the tiny desert emirate. There were Armenians, whose ancient lands had been confiscated by the Ottomans – itinerant craftsmen whose ancestors had wandered the Arab world with nothing, but who now crafted exquisite jewels for the super-rich. There were also Syrian car mechanics, Egyptian caretakers, Indian accountants, Danish ice-cream manufacturers, American diplomats and, of course, many, many oil workers.

Saturday to Wednesday we were fully occupied with school, Friday was church, but Thursday was our day to explore. This became a lot easier once we were able to buy a car. Kuwait itself did not hold much for the intrepid explorer. Being a flat desert mostly of gritty sand, about the same size as the state of New Jersey in the US or just a bit smaller than Wales, you could drive round it in a day. The population was almost exclusively housed in Kuwait City and its surrounding conurbation. Little was left of the pre-oil kingdom – only the merest glimpses of the fishing culture in the *dhow* boatyards of Fahaheel, and small communities of Bedouin still preferring a life under canvas to the breeze-block walls of the town. A few traditional *Bayt Cha'er* – low-slung black goatswool tents – could occasionally be found, but were always completed with a noisy generator and pick-up truck outside. The coast, however, was different. Kuwait Bay is a wide expanse of mud refreshed twice daily by the tide, bringing rich feeding for the cormorants, flamingos, herons and a host of waders – particularly in winter. Towards the south, uninterrupted white sandy beaches called us, fringing the piercingly blue waters of the Gulf.

But it was further afield that we looked for adventure – with school holidays at our disposal, Egypt and North Africa beckoned. Egypt was definitely top of the list of the "must see" places. Expats seemed divided after that – one group favouring the shopping experiences of Bahrain and Dubai, with the major alternative being the desert landscapes and history of Jordan and Morocco. A few intrepid explorers recommended Syria but no one we knew had been to the closest adventurous location – Iraq. The reason was simple; with the Iran/Iraq war raging for most of the previous decade, the ultimate Middle Eastern itinerary, taking in the crucible of civilization, was out of bounds. But all of that changed as the border was reopened to tourists and the first trickle entered from Kuwait in late 1989 and early 1990. We made plans!

With our friends Marianne and Stephen, we loaded up our four-wheel drive jeep and set off immediately at the end of school, at the National Day holiday in February. Wanting to maximize the four-day weekend, we made good time to the Iraqi border, passing the colossal oil wells illuminating the night-time desert of northern Kuwait with their pulsating orange flares. Smooth progress continued at the Kuwaiti exit post but ran into the Iraqi sand as a labyrinthine border process unfolded, with Iraqi officials housed in small semi-derelict huts alternately barking orders or fastidiously ignoring all human communication. Seven hours later we had somehow performed all the tasks assigned to us, as evidenced by the stamps in our passports. Unfortunately the said passports were in the hands of yet another border guard who would rifle through the pages one at a time and then, having established the nationality of the document, throw it into the assembled crowd with the cry of *"French"*, *"Suuri"* or in our happy case, *"Britch"*.

And so we headed to Basra. We were hopelessly late for our reservations at the hotel, and in great need of a bed for the night. We quickly lowered our search criteria for acceptance of new hotels and found two small establishments that would shelter two "Britch" couples. This was no mean feat as Marianne has a pathological fear of insects and "no visible cockroaches" had been one of the original criteria. With so little time for the vast country ahead of us, we left Basra early and drove north to Baghdad first thing the next morning.

What struck me most forcibly was the countryside of Iraq. Here was the desert of Kuwait but with a huge difference – rivers! First the Shatt el Arab, the confluence of Iraq's great rivers, and then the Euphrates itself. For much of the journey, the sands were unaffected by the presence of these waterways, constrained as they were to linear conduits slicing through the landscape. But in places a more ancient pattern remained, with large areas of reed, open water and mud, hosting thriving communities of water birds and the *Madan*, the Marsh Arabs in their villages built of rushes. The productivity of the land was evidenced by the enormous flocks of ducks, coots and herons, and the water buffalo ploughing sodden furrows, trucks laden with vegetables and wayside stalls selling fruit. As we travelled north this organic landscape became less common, but the life-giving nature of the river was still obvious in the neat acres of green where it was used to irrigate plantations of dates.

My worst experience was filling the car with petrol. In this land of oil, petrol was cheaper than water – and used with similar abandon. Having removed the car's petrol cap, the attendant pulled the hose from the pump and started distributing the fuel over me, the car bonnet and eventually into the fuel tank. As I jumped back and protested, he laughed between teeth clenching a lighted cigarette. Realizing a discussion on health and safety would not get me far – even if I could speak Arabic – I took a change of clothes from the back of the jeep and retreated to the small hut which served as a toilet. Here I was grateful that the petrol fumes masked, to a limited extent at least, the stench of the facility.

Baghdad was a city under a cloud. Brilliant sunshine, palm trees and the lapis blue of the minarets could not dispel the gloom. It infected the nervous greetings of our hotel hosts and the strained interactions with the taxi drivers. It was epitomized by the main decoration in the hotel lobby where we were staying. A full-sized cardboard cut-out of a middle-aged man in full military fatigues appeared from the opening curtains of a mock stage – Saddam Hussein. Despite the cloud, the locals we met were passionately hospitable and keen to hear news of the outside world. Conversations with the urbane and sophisticated Iraqis were full of Paris and London but went embarrassingly quiet if we asked about life in the republic.

Babylon – even the name is iconic; the world heritage site, like the nation, is a contradiction of a unique culture and the personal aggrandizement of one man. It is home to such world treasures as the Ishtar Gate, the eroded stump of the tower of Babel and the place of Hammurabi's code. As we entered the site we passed a huge banner. On the left characteristic wedge-shaped marks of cuneiform flowed from the profile of Nebuchadnezzar into Arabic script and the image of Saddam – the message was clear.

The Euphrates glides southwards below the brick fields of the ancient ziggurat famed as the tower of Babel. From the mound it looked so easy to reach the place where we could recite the words from Psalm 137 beloved by Bob Marley and Boney M, but just as the ancient Israelites were in a strange land, so were we. What looked like the setting for the perfect tourist picture turned out to be a military installation under cover of palm trees. The officer who verified we were indeed lost tourists was gracious but firm, and as a result we had fewer snaps from the ruins as he ripped the film from the camera.

On our return south we were to meet the military again – in rather different circumstances. Driving along the nearly empty desert highway, miles from anywhere, we were overtaken by an articulated lorry. Just as its back wheels drew alongside us, it swerved to narrow the gap. As it sailed past I lost all control of the jeep and, at around seventy miles per hour, careered into the sand dune running along the roadside. We had noticed the knives sticking out from the hub caps of many of the trucks, Boudicca-style, previously, but had not appreciated their purpose till this point – to keep rival vehicles at a distance while overtaking, with tyre-shredding consequences if they did not give way sufficiently. After it dawned on us what had happened, we were left incredulous at the side of the road, the jeep half-buried in sand.

Even while we scratched our heads, a half-dozen or so Iraqi soldiers appeared as from nowhere, manually dragged the jeep out of the sand, lifted the frame and changed the wheel. Barely pausing for us to thank them, they were gone as quickly as they had come. As well as thanking our military guardian angels, we realized there were *a lot* of soldiers in Iraq.

Our brief trip to Iraq underlined the feeling that although we had begun to understand something of the international culture surrounding the school, we knew almost nothing of the Kuwaiti way of life. In Baghdad, if only briefly, we had learned a little about how Iraqis went about their daily lives, what concerned them, and how they viewed the outside world. These insights had come through conversations as we exchanged stories with our hosts, the owners of the hotel. Kuwaitis, insulated by wealth and a minority in their own country, kept themselves apart. However, a connection opened up for us into the conservative cocoon of Kuwaiti family life in an unexpected and dramatic way shortly after our Iraq trip.

In the early hours of a March morning, Susanna woke with paralysing pains in her lower abdomen. Forbidden to go with her in

32

the ambulance, I followed in our car. Important as it was to arrive at the government hospital to admit Susanna, as a male relative was required for the admissions process, I was not allowed to pass reception, as this was a women's hospital and men were only permitted in the afternoon visiting hour. I was allowed to wait until a doctor emerged to tell me that nothing would be done during the night shift and I was to return the next day.

For me, the following days were a limbo of worry and brief encounters with Susanna – visiting under the rigorous schedule of the ward. In brief conversations I would learn of the tests carried out and the most recent theories of the medical staff. With some alarm I left after visiting on the third day with the news that if a pregnancy test came back positive it was an ectopic pregnancy and they would operate the next day. Worried that the doctors were jumping to over-hasty conclusions, I was determined to get a second opinion – at least by proxy.

Talking through the sequence of events with medical friends from church, our suspicions were confirmed – any such diagnosis would be premature. The news at the next visiting time that we were expecting a baby was not the great news that we had always hoped it would be. However, we did not agree with the doctors that the life needed to be lost as soon as possible and that Susanna should be immediately prepared for emergency surgery. Instead, having been given all the papers and medical test results in her patient file and told to book her into the surgical ward, we waited till the medics left. Under cover of the hubbub of family visiting time, Susanna climbed out of the window, meeting me at the strategically parked car. We drove a few miles to a private hospital where I had arranged for a second consultation. Here we received the delightful news that Susanna had an ovarian cyst – which should be no danger to her early but normal pregnancy.

Prior to our flight, Susanna had experienced something of life behind the veil for the Kuwaiti women in the ward. Although I saw a flock of sombre birds, cloaked as the women were by the full *abiyah* and veil, as soon as the visiting hour was over their true Kuwaiti plumage emerged. Once the danger of non-relative male eyes seeing an inch of skin had gone, the black curtains were drawn back and the sun came out. The brightly coloured and sequined clothes were only one part of the transformation. Susanna told me that the women's behaviour changed as dramatically as their garments. In an obstetrics and gynaecology ward, the full panoply of human experience is laid bare – joy with new life and the deep grief of loss. A sisterhood of patients supported one another – sharing with neighbour-strangers the most intimate details, tears, hugs and love.

As a Western patient in a government hospital, Susanna was unusual and attracted quizzical interest. She had placed a picture of me next to her bed, much to the delight and amusement of the Kuwaiti women. When, on one occasion, I kissed her prior to departure, at the end of the visiting hour, the action was greeted with a round of applause and, after my departure, when the visits were dissected by the ward matriarchs, Susanna learned a lot about Kuwaiti marriages. In contrast to the Western pattern, many Kuwaiti women find their deepest friendships and support in female relatives and friends. The thought that your best friend might be your husband was bizarre in the extreme.

Our brief hospital encounter started a process that would carry on – getting to know the Arab culture from the inside. To me, who could only see the *abiyah* and veil, the women appeared impersonal, cold and aloof. They could not look me in the eye and would remove their hand if I extended mine in greeting. But Susanna had entered their world and found a reality far removed from this superficial impression. The Middle East was beginning to beguile us with its mysterious beauty. While it was not always easy to appreciate on the surface, we had glimpsed, through its wrappings, something of its colour, texture and warmth.

As the brief spring melted into summer, our thoughts turned increasingly to home. With thoughts of England's green fields, family, and a pint at the pub, we made preparations for a short UK holiday before returning for the next academic year in the Gulf. On arrival, we experienced a drop of 30 degrees C to what seemed the cool 25 degrees C of a good English summer.

Shortly after, in desolation, we returned to hospital as Susanna miscarried our first child. After convalescence and time with our families, we determined to experience the full restorative beauty of "green" and so set off for a holiday to the Outer Hebrides. It was while en route that we heard the world-stopping news that Iraqi troops had invaded Kuwait. It made no sense. There had been no warning. Why? How were our friends? What would happen to our apartment, our belongings? What next for the country, for us?

No one had any answers, but we recognized the need to go south as soon as possible. Kuwaiti assets were about to be frozen and the only UK branch of the National Bank of Kuwait that held all our worldly wealth was in London. They were allowing withdrawals of up to £1,000 a day. We got there in time for one withdrawal before the accounts were frozen, by which time we realized, with the rest of the world, that looted and occupied Kuwait would never be the same again and we were very unlikely to return.

August is not a good time to be an unemployed teacher. As soon as head teachers returned to their desks late in the month, we started the search for temporary work. At different ends of the spectrum, Susanna got a job in a prep school in Oxford and I commuted to Tower Hamlets for a supply post in a large comprehensive school.

As we slowly put our own lives back together, every night, horrified, we watched the pictures coming out of Kuwait. Our neighbourhood was overrun with troops, Kuwaitis were being summarily executed, Westerners had either gone into hiding or been taken as captives to Baghdad. As a society we are inured to pictures of war – they are a nightly spectacle beamed into our living rooms. When these sights are coming from your street, your shopping centres, your school, then the truth hits. War is horrific and it is the ordinary citizens who suffer most – people just like us. One image more than any other captured the pain of our separation and anxiety over the fate of Kuwait and its people; the figure of a vulnerable five-year-old British schoolboy, his hair ruffled by the Butcher of Baghdad, grabbed media headlines and brought down the wrath of the international community. For Susanna, he was one of the children in the classroom next door.

Autumn turned to winter. The numbers of Western troops in Saudi Arabia grew and the rhetoric from Iraq became more bellicose, the two sides squaring up for war. Like two rival stags, the posturing lasted far longer than the conflict as, despite near-equal numbers, this was to be no equal contest. Although we prayed for the deliverance of Kuwait, news from the battlefields left us chilled. Leaving behind a looted and broken city, large numbers of ill-equipped Iraqi troops surrendered, many without boots. Others fled, only to be annihilated in their thousands by massive air strikes on their retreating convoys. Mutla Ridge, which we knew as a scenic picnic spot, became the dying grounds for two Iraqi divisions. The carbonized corpses melded to the tanks, army trucks and stolen cars, limousines and fire engines carrying the pickings of a sacked city. Is this where our stolen jeep met its end? And what about the conscripts who had rescued us, barely a year earlier, from the sands just a few kilometres up the same road? Were they incinerated as they fled?

It was over. Kuwait had been liberated. In the coming months, some friends would return to help rebuild the country, but we had new jobs, a new home and a new child on the way. Often, when people asked what it was like to lose everything in such a dramatic way, we would honestly be able to say that what we had lost, God had given us back. Of our personal possessions nothing remained (our apartment building had been completely looted by the retreating Iraqi army), but through the generosity of friends and family and renewed employment, we had a furnished home again.

The only thing we really missed – the one thing that we felt was irreplaceable – was our wedding album. One day, on returning from school to our new home in Lincoln, a package was waiting for us – inside the house, the front door locked and the parcel without any stamps. The white and gold folder was sandy and had the clear imprint of a soldier's boot on its cover, but it was our wedding album. We heard God saying: "I hear – I know."

It took us three restorative years before we felt ready to return to the Arab world. In many ways, even now, it is still recovering from the events of the early 1990s. Events still far in the future were to trace their beginnings to the Gulf deserts with Western armies encamped to protect the international trade of oil. But that was all still to come and several countries later.

CHAPTER 2

The Keys to the House:
The Arabic Language

1994–95
Amman, Jordan

The church might not seem the obvious vehicle for a return trip to the Arab world, seen as it is by many as a Western institution. The reality is that it has oriental roots. God conducted his discourse with the world in Mesopotamia, Egypt and Palestine. Jesus spoke Aramaic (a language still spoken in a few remote Syrian villages), and it was from the founding churches of these lands that Christianity spread. During the years in the UK, following our brush with the Arabian Gulf, we became more and more convinced that we should return, but we realized that we needed to be better prepared a second time around. We wanted to receive from and give to Arabia. We were not precisely sure what or how – but we were ready to give of our time and talents where they could be best deployed, and knew that our lives would be the richer for it.

Practically, to put ourselves at the service of the church, we needed to do two things. The first was to join a cross-cultural Christian organization that worked to place personnel with the national churches of the region. (We joined Interserve, an organization with a history of over 150 years of partnering with churches in the Middle East and Asia.) Secondly, we needed to learn Arabic, and that is where Jordan came in. After a rather emotional series of goodbyes, we arrived in Amman in time for the new term at the language school.

Amman is built on a series of hills that brood over the central souq and commercial district, complete with its Roman amphitheatre and antique arches. Connected by snaking steps for pedestrians and switchback streets for cars, each hillside is densely packed with three and four-storey apartment blocks, all faced with the same white limestone that dictates the contours of the landscape. We lived on the *Jabal* (hill) Amman, close to the language school in a block of flats delighting in the address: "*Bayt* Mohammed, on the steps near the Safidee Mosque, first circle, *Jabal* Amman". First circle in the address referred to the roundabout system extending from the older neighbourhood of our area to the newer, grander suburbs, until one reached the villas of the seventh circle and the road to the airport.

The language school did not have a childcare programme and so our most urgent task before school started was to sort out provision for Sam (just two) and Chloe (a baby of nine months). We were quickly connected to the extended church and expat networks and rather nervously arranged for Sam to attend an Arabic/English nursery and for Chloe to be childminded, along with the baby of some American students. Sam, an inquisitive and mischievous child, thrived on new experiences and quickly made friends. Despite Chloe's initial separation anxiety, we built up a family rhythm that worked for the children and our language learning. There is an undoubted correlation here; the younger the children, the easier it is for families to adapt and settle cross-culturally.

The few days prior to language school also gave us the opportunity to explore something of Amman. With no car but living quite centrally, we took full advantage of those steps – hundreds and hundreds of them – walking down to the throng and hubbub of the souq, but usually taking a taxi back. For a few coins we would squeeze into the back seats of a large Mercedes saloon and, after the driver had packed in another three or four passengers, the overloaded car would snake its way up the hill, dropping us at the first circle. Locally known as Rainbow Street, after the convenience store on the corner, this once grand road was an eclectic mix of buildings. The Saudi embassy was locked behind high walls and forbidding doors, opposite a derelict cinema. *Falafel* take-out stalls and discount stores jostled with boutique fashion outlets that rarely opened. Off this main street, there were fine old houses; crumbling, single-storey grandeur hiding cool green courtyards. The white stone walls served as a palette to the hot vibrancy of the bougainvillea and the cool green and yellow of the lemon trees.

As we settled into our neighbourhood, even before it became homework, we realized that visiting the neighbours was a large part of our communal responsibility. Both neighbourhood boundaries and obligations seemed tightly defined. We were part of a territory comprising six or seven apartment blocks, up and down the communal steps and dominated by Um and Abu Mohammed and Um and Abu Helmi.

Abu Mohammed was our landlord and clearly the wealthiest member of the community. This gave his wife, Um Mohammed, huge social reach. Abu Helmi, the local taxi driver, was the most religious of the local patriarchs and this gave Um Helmi great status. Around these two pivotal families were uncles, aunts, cousins, children, grandchildren, tenants, and foreign language students with two cute blond kids (ours). On returning to the apartment from a family errand, calls to come and visit were always warm and friendly, and if we had the children with us, insistent. Despite our lack of Arabic, the piping hot sweet tea, fruit and pastries would keep the social etiquette flowing and the children the centre of attention.

This was not always received well by the kids, however. Particularly for Sam, sweets were all well and good, but pinched cheeks and the constant refrain of *"Habibi"* (my loved one) would quickly engender his angry retort, complete with a well-aimed punch – "I'm not a baby!" At this point, our hosts would fall about with laughter. This would encourage further outbursts of anger from our now out-of-control two-year-old. Unless we were feeling particularly cross-culturally strong, we did not usually visit with Sam!

Unexpectedly, language school itself was another cross-cultural experience. Divided into semesters, a new programme started every six months. Each new cohort of around thirty students was further divided into classes of about ten. With Susanna, I was in a class made up of three other couples and several singles: American, Canadian, a South Korean, another Brit and a Ukrainian. All wanting to learn Arabic, we were a mixed bag of abilities, which brought fascinating national characteristics to light. The philosophy of the language school was a mixture of language drills – repetitive chants, the learning of long lists of vocab – and as much social visiting with neighbours as possible.

Progress for most of us was painfully slow, and made even more difficult by the quickness of a few. Although culture shock and family logistics meant a pedestrian progress for many, others with more time to visit, previous experience, or just more language aptitude became increasingly frustrated with the speed of the class. Often by the last session of the day, friction would surface. One lightning rod for stress discharge was the weekly homework chart. The administration asked us all to fill in and sign how many hours we had spent that week in study and visiting. Nothing was done with the information – we were fee-paying students and in no danger of losing our places – but as a motivation it clearly did not work for us all. After a particularly discouraging lesson of Arabic dictation, production of the chart was sure to set sparks flying. Interestingly, Europeans (usually led by stroppy Brits) would near-universally refuse to sign up to how much study they were doing. North Americans, however, found this truculent behaviour disturbingly disrespectful. Our Jordanian teachers were quite unbothered by either response, reciting the mantra, "It is up to you, but the more you study the quicker you will learn."

Humour was another divider. Again, in our class, we were split by the Atlantic. As we struggled with Arabic verb conjunctions, tension became palpable and the slightest humorous slip could send half of us into hysterics. The more we were glared at, with the question, "Why are you wasting our time?" written into the look, the more difficult it was to stop. On one particular occasion, when our delightful young female teacher pronounced in her best but very broken English a story about the land of a monarch as "the king's condom" we were apoplectic and had to have an early tea break to prevent the lesson dissolving into farce. Despite our lapses we did make slow progress. What at first exposure seemed to be a string of random sounds slowly revealed its pattern. Syllables coalesced into words; intonation revealed intention, and occasionally we recognized meaning.

There is nothing quite like language learning. From the life of hectic teachers with a thousand things to do each day, busy with friends, family and church, we now had one task (and two small children). The task was to learn to speak. I hadn't done this successfully since I was a toddler. At secondary school I had proved I no longer had the ability as I shredded the French language three times a week. Now, eight hours a day, we were studying; learning grammar, reciting vocabulary, memorizing dictations, and deciphering the foreign text. When we weren't studying we were visiting, listening; absorbing the sounds of a region. It was immersion in Arabic. Slowly, by osmosis, understanding seeped in, but it wasn't a steady flow. We lurched in understanding, with breakthroughs followed by disappointing plateaux when nothing new seemed to go in.

For me, Arabic grammar was one area that was resistant to assimilation. A product of the 1960s British elementary schooling, I had little handle on the formal structure of English grammar, so lectures, introducing the labyrinthine rules of noun cases, split plurals, past and non-past paradigms of verbs left me floundering with the English labels, let alone the Arabic examples. But slowly a language ocean, deep and ancient, still full of mysteries, yes, but also exquisitely beautiful, spread out before us. Rather like our brief family trips to the Red Sea coral reefs along the Jordanian coast, we were snorkelling, submerged only to a depth of a few metres but able to glimpse the kaleidoscope wonder of this new world.

Our snorkel safaris (an Arabic word) into the language revealed an ecosystem populated with complex, highly evolved forms. We came across the "nonconcatenative" root system, sounding like an obscure invertebrate phylum, but in reality the elegant design underlying the building blocks of the living words. Arabic words all come from three letter roots – always consonants. When fitted with vowels, they make words, linked by concept. Topping and tailing changes the meaning but retains the family resemblance.

An example might help: *k- t- b* is the essence of "write". Separate the consonants with the vowel "a" and you have "he wrote" (*katab*); continue by finishing with *tu* and it becomes "I wrote" (*katabtu*). Double the middle *t* and it becomes "I had something written" (*kattabtu*), shorten and change the vowels and you have "I dictate" (*uktibu*). Showing this powerful force is not limited to verbs; *kitaab* is book, *kaatib* is writer, *maktab* is desk and *maktaba* is bookshop.

But I am getting ahead of myself. The most basic building blocks of the web of words are sounds, represented by letters. Arabic has twenty-eight; twenty-five of them consonants and three written vowels. Arabic speakers are very forgiving when it comes to vowels and words slide between dialects and regions around the a, the i and the u sounds. So "boy" may be *walad* or *wilid*, or something in between. So cursory is the attitude to the short vowels that they are not even written in most texts. The consonants conjoin, leaving space only in reading primers and formal missives for a semaphore-style notation of dashes that enable pronunciation.

Not so the consonants! There is no latitude here. Most of the sounds are also fundamental to English, such as s, b and r (although that one is more like the rolled Scots "r" than the English). But others are unknown to the Western ear. Here are the sounds that give most trouble to the English-speaking language student:

- "Kh" sounds like you are politely clearing your throat.

- "Ain" often at the start of words transliterated with an initial "A" like in "Arabic" itself. Just imagine saying "Arabic" with a spoon pushing down the back of your tongue.

- "The Hamza" is a glottal stop, like the good old cockney "bo'le" (bottle).

- "Dal" is a close approximation to Homer Simpson's "d" in "Doh!"

These and other letters are coded not by the Roman alphabet but by the Arabic *Abjad* script, flowing from the back of a book to the front (from an English perspective) and from right to left on the page. The text is fluid, one letter flowing into the next. Its innate artistry has long been exploited, and calligraphy has reached its highest forms with these cursive strokes. A surprise and a big difference to English – it is really quite easy to learn to read Arabic! Purely phonetic with logical spelling, decoding the text is a simple task – though understanding what you have read is more complicated.

Reading as a tool to language learning poses a particular problem to the student of Arabic. Spoken language is always a variant of the formal written form – just think how different the TV newsreader sounds to the teenager on their mobile phone. But with Arabic, the differences are much greater. Across the Arab world, Modern Standard Arabic is used in written and formal communication. A well-educated resident of Marrakesh or Baghdad could read the same newspaper but, if they met to chat, they would have great difficulty in understanding one another. Written Arabic preserves the pedigree of the language; Arabic

45

spoken in Jordan is flexible and has changed through time and culture to diverge from its classical roots and other dialects. For the language student it gives a dilemma – do you learn the spoken form, the written form or both? The best answer is to learn both. Written Arabic is foundational to understanding the colloquial, crucial to being able to adapt to new dialects, and essential if you want to learn to read.

So obviously I decided to learn spoken Arabic only – that was going to be stretch enough for me!

When it came to our dictation homework, we took a leaf out of the local teenagers' books as we paced backwards and forwards for hours, noses stuck in our texts, muttering to ourselves over and over, searing the words into our memories. Much of our study was like this – isolated, focused and dull – but much more was embedded in the community and landscape. Just walking to the school was a language experience. I loved the routine, the streets, the noise, the heat, and smells. Each morning, Susanna would wind her way up to "Little Stars" with Sam. The nursery was set in an old colonial house, with glistening white stone walls and red-tiled roof shaded by loquat and lemon trees, a toddlers' United Nations with children of parents from all over the globe. Meanwhile, I would take a service taxi to second circle with Chloe, from where we would walk in the shade of the oleander trees to her childminder and baby friend. Throughout our years in the Middle East, outside the home, the children were exposed to far more American English than British; perhaps it was this early start that gave Chloe the American twang that has stuck with her.

There were always conversations in the taxi, everyone loved Chloe, the baby on my knee, but it was the walk home after a morning of language lessons that I really enjoyed. Chloe, strapped into the backpack, chattering on, was my walking companion into an assault on the senses. The lunchtime prayer call would start, first from one mosque and then from all points of the compass. Slightly out of time, the nasal chant would rise to a crescendo, punctuated by a litany of car horns and underscored by the glossolalia of the flood of schoolchildren disgorging from the secondary school on our route home. At the start of the journey, heady scents from jasmine and orange blossom, hidden behind high walls in the gardens of the upmarket villas, intoxicated the air. By the time I had reached first circle I was hungry, as the smell of sizzling *falafel* and grilled chicken *shawerma* reminded me of how long it had been since breakfast. The fierce light picked out every colour: the dome of the Abdali mosque, pigeon-egg blue in the distance, and the Phoenician purple of the jacaranda trees, complete with sunbirds, living jewels, iridescent in the foliage.

It was on a sensory high that returning to the flat one morning, I had a startling conversation with Susanna.

"I love walking around our neighbourhood, I love the streets, the sounds, the smells. Everyone is so friendly."

"That's funny, I hate it!" came the unexpected reply.

"What! Why? You are always so positive about our neighbours."

"Yes, but that isn't what you are talking about. I hate walking up to the shops, picking up Sam, just going down the steps outside the building – because I get hassled."

Susanna was clearly agitated and I realized I had missed something that had been building for a while. I needed to tread carefully, but I wasn't going to be given a chance for calming words just yet.

"It's OK for you. You're a man."

This sounded like an accusation. Best to keep quiet and let her finish.

"If I were to go out now and walk to the corner shop, I would have men crossing the street so they can "brush past me", ribald comments from groups of young men on the street corner, and I would be followed home."

I was shocked. How come I hadn't noticed? "But I've never seen any of this," I said, puzzled.

"Of course you haven't. When I walk with you, it doesn't happen – only when I am on my own or with the kids."

We were clearly living in two quite different worlds. To help me understand hers, Susanna suggested an experiment. The next day we took a walk, but rather than walking together, she walked ahead and I hung back, following on the opposite side of the road.

The test lasted less than five minutes. I couldn't take it any longer. I nearly came to blows with a middle-aged man who tried to block Susanna's path, making her walk off the pavement and into the road to avoid his lecherous advances.

Back in the apartment, Susanna looked smug.

"How do you cope?" I blurted out as we shut the door on the collision of our two worlds.

"I make sure I am always covered up when I go outside, avoid any eye contact, ignore the comments and use the Arabic phrases our language teachers taught us if it gets intense."

"Like what?"

"Like – 'Would you say that to your sister?' or 'Where is your mother?' Or I just shout 'shame on you'. That usually does the trick."

This is hardly a problem unique to the streets of Amman, nor to foreign women. This was brought home to us dramatically through our friendship with Zeinab, Susanna's language tutor. It was becoming increasingly difficult for Susanna to attend language school full-time and keep the family sane. Of the two of us she is also the better linguist, so after the first semester we decided that I would stay at the language school and that Susanna would study, part-time, with the help of a local tutor, and so Zeinab came into our lives. She was one of the godliest, most humble and helpful people we knew. A devout Muslim from a family of four sisters, she earned much of the household income by tutoring foreigners, her father having abandoned the family many years before.

Now, we need to consider the subject of the *hijab* for the purpose of this narrative, but also it is one of those lightning rod issues that are picked up again and again as a key divider, and given great importance in Western news media. As an example, in the week that I was writing this chapter, there were two separate headline stories (in the top three of the BBC *News at Six*) about the Muslim headscarf and face covering.[3]

Veiling predates Islam and can be traced through Christian tradition and practice in the region. From ancient times, respectable Greek and Roman women covered themselves with a sheet when in the street.[4] In seventh-century Arabia, prior to Islam, veiling was unknown, but in Damascus and other Byzantine cities it was reserved as a privilege of the upper classes. Mohammed's wives and the other early Muslim women adopted the custom, as is indicated in the Qur'an (33:59):

O Prophet, tell your wives, your daughters and women believers to wrap their outer garments closely around them, for this makes it more likely that they will be recognised and not be harassed. God is All Forgiving, Compassionate to each.[5]

This was once a token that united women of good character, a social identifier marking out respectable women. In the New Testament book of 1 Corinthians, in a passage difficult to understand as our cultural references have shifted so dramatically, Paul identifies Christian women's head covering as normative in worship: "But every woman who prays or prophesies with her head uncovered dishonours her head – it is the same as having her head shaved."[6]

A nun's wimple and cornette echo these early social mores, preserving Christian *hijab* from an ancient root. Even today Christian women in many congregations around the Middle East put on lacy headscarves when they enter church or take communion.

---

[3] One story concerned NHS staff wearing the *niqab* (full face covering). Patients polled clearly indicated that they wanted to see the face of the medical staff treating them. However, the news report was unable to find a practising doctor or nurse who covered their face while working. The second was a ruling that when giving evidence, witnesses in a British court must remove their face covering.

[4] Christine A. Mallouhi, *Mini-Skirts, Mothers and Muslims* Oxford: Monarch Books, 2004, p. 49.

[5] Tarif Khaldi, *The Qur'an: A New Translation*, London: Penguin, 2009, p. 344.

[6] 1 Corinthians 11:5, NIV, UK 2011.

The passage referred to from the Qur'an hints at why many contemporary Muslim women cover up. Positively, it is so that they will be "recognised" and negatively, so that they won't be "harassed". Suzanne Haneef explores the former when she writes:

> *hijab is not an isolated aspect of the Muslim women's life but fits in with and reinforces the Islamic social system, and in particular the Islamic concept of womanhood. Just as Western forms of dress have developed from and fit the Western world view, societal values and conception of womanhood of Western civilisation, so does the dress of Muslim women emanate from and fit the Islamic value system and view of life.*[7]

Perhaps this is why the wearing of *hijab* has become such a hot topic. It is a very obvious, impossible to miss statement of belonging to a particular worldview. This can be established at an individual, family, or community level. A Muslim family or community can mark out its identity through the way its women dress as much as any individual woman can so choose to self-identify. We knew families where both men and women made it plain by their appearance that they were Muslim. For the women, it meant wearing *hijab*. For the men, it meant flowing beards, often without a moustache, with a permanent mark on the forehead from the repeated obeisance, head touching the ground, through the prayer ritual. We also knew families where Muslim identity was clearly demonstrated through the women's head covering and the men gave nothing away by their outward appearance.

The Arabic word "*hijab*" literally means a screen or a curtain. As well as being an identifier and a mark of respect, there is a real sense in which the covering hides the wearer. In male-dominated societies this gives women tremendous freedom. Given immunity

---

[7] Suzanne Haneef, *What Everyone Should Know About Islam and Muslims*, Chicago, IL: Kazi Publications, 1979, p. 168.

from being looked at in a sexual way, she is able to face the world as an individual. Suzanne Haneef explains:

> *this modest attire protects the Muslim woman from the sexual interest and improper looks and behaviour of men; wearing it she can move about in the world as necessity requires with dignity and a complete consciousness of her own propriety and modesty.*[8]

As the Qur'an puts it – "they will … not be harassed".

Or will they?

Zeinab was always dressed modestly. She would enter our apartment, whatever the weather, enrobed in a full-length coat. With sleeves to the wrist and hem to her shoes, it covered a similarly proportioned dress. The high collar came up to her tightly fitting headscarf, kept in place with a discreet pin. Not a lock of hair could escape to a male gaze. Her dress really was an extension of her. She was always the height of modesty and respectability. Coming from a simple house and poor neighbourhood, she travelled freely on the public transport, head held high with a firm contentedness. In her own house, with her family, she was behind the curtain and so the *hijab* would come off and she could be truly relaxed. In our house with me in attendance and unknown visitors likely to drop by, only her overcoat would be removed.

With the contralto notes of legendary Umm Kulthum, heavy as the scent of jasmine, drifting down from our neighbours above, Susanna was waiting at the table, dictionaries, Arabic grammar primers and notebooks at the ready. The afternoon was hot, the children drowsily watching a *Thomas the Tank Engine* video on the TV screen. Unusually, Zeinab was late. Suddenly the lazy afternoon was shattered as a despairing wail cut through the music, followed by a slap on the front door. We were galvanized into action. I leapt for the door, wrenching it open to reveal Zeinab's crumpled form sobbing on the step. I took chase after the attacker, first glancing

---

[8] Haneef, *What Everyone Should Know About Islam and Muslims*, p. 170.

down at our distraught friend. I didn't catch him, my speed hampered by running barefoot (like our neighbours, we never wore shoes in the house).

Seared into my memory from that sultry afternoon is the sight of Zeinab, exposed on the doorstep. Her attacker had only managed to rip away her headscarf, but to me the exposed hair tumbling over her tear-soaked face was a violent nakedness. Zeinab's private world had been invaded, her curtain torn down. I stayed out of the way long enough for Susanna to comfort our trampled language teacher and friend, knowing that by the time I got back, her *hijab* would be back in place, her curtain restored to where it should be.

We had been learning the language for months and were both able to function pretty effectively in Arabic in most simple social contexts. Very little of our conversation practice was carried out jointly, and so although we could both happily do the shopping, talk about church, and explain why we were studying Arabic, from there on our vocabulary diverged according to our male and female neighbours' preoccupations. Susanna could talk about the children and extended families, mastering the complexities of nouns describing relatives to the nth connection. Much more usefully, I could talk football and was able to use the ubiquitous knowledge of the Premier League to talk about English geography: "Yes, I grew up in a town quite near Arsenal."

As our language proficiency progressed, the question that grew in our minds was, where next? We had assumed that we would go back to the Arabian Gulf; Bahrain, the UAE or Oman perhaps. We had visited Oman for a conference and fell in love with the brown serrated hills thrusting out of the cream-coloured, sandy plains. The twentieth-century infrastructure alongside Bedouin tradition and coral reefs offshore were all very appealing. There were also plenty of opportunities for teachers in the numerous International schools.

As the question grew, so did the frequency of a dream that returned to Susanna almost nightly. It was always the same. I knew it as well as her, as every morning she would repeat it, never changing. We were living in an old house, red-roofed, with a very particular and ornate ceiling. The house was set on its own on a green hillside, which rose to a high peak and descended to the sea. Around the nearby houses were well-tended gardens with neat rows of vegetables in the shade of fruit trees, overburdened with oranges, peaches, and lemons. Within this very non-Arabian vision, Susanna had a great sense of peace, with a clear sense that this was where God wanted us to live.

I never had the dream, but one day when I picked up the post for our colleagues at the language school and set off home looking at the envelopes, I was hit with a force of recognition. I came across a postcard addressed to a friend and saw Susanna's dream! Quickly turning the card over, I scanned for the place name. It was simply captioned "The hills above Beirut". I rushed home and have to confess that I showed the card to Susanna before delivering it to its rightful owner.

"What do you think of this?" I said, holding the card for Susanna to see.

"It's my dream, exactly, even to the number of houses, how they fit into the scenery and the type of trees! Where is it?" With shaking hands, she turned over the card.

"Lebanon! But I told God – pretty well anywhere, but not Lebanon."

"Perhaps that is why God gave you the dream and not me."

"But Interserve doesn't even have anyone in Lebanon… does it?"

We agreed that we should find out. To understand why Susanna was so reluctant, we need to rewind a few years back from 1994 when Susanna had the dream. It was only late in 1991 that Terry Waite had been released from his near five-year captivity at the hands of a Lebanese militia. The long years of civil war only ended in 1990. Growing up in the 1970s and 80s, Beirut was a byword for urban warfare. Grainy scenes of guerrillas fighting over a devastated wasteland was our nightly news fare. We knew God used dreams in the Bible; Joseph comes to mind, and we had even been told that interpretation of dreams was important in some contemporary Middle Eastern cultures.

But, for us?

We had to find out. So we asked our area director and discovered that there was a very small team in Lebanon that they were looking to enlarge. What is more, they wanted teachers as, post-war, many schools were asking for expertise from qualified staff, particularly if they spoke English.

Message received!

CHAPTER 3

Lebanon After the Civil War

1995–97
Qab Elias, the Bekaa, Lebanon

Beirut Airport looked like a James Bond set – after the action of
the movie had rearranged the concrete pillars and pockmarked the
walls. Despite our voluminous luggage, we were quickly through
the arrival formalities and greeted by a driver from the school where
we were to start our missionary career. In a sleepy daze we sped
through the late-night Beirut streets and up onto the Damascus
highway that took us from the narrow, city-dominated coastal strip,
up and over the mountains to the Bekaa plain, the rural hinterland
of Lebanon and home for the next six years.

We were going to live in *Bayt Kassis* in the Bekaa town of Qab
Elias. In a few weeks I would start teaching at the secondary
Evangelical School in the regional capital of Zahle, ten miles to
the north. In Qab Elias, its much smaller sister school had a vacant
apartment, traditionally used by the pastor of the associated church
– hence the name (*Bayt* = house, *Kassis* = pastor). Perched like an
eagle's eyrie in the old quarter of the town, it had a magnificent
view over the sprawling streets, the sweeping Bekaa plain and
across to the Syrian heights of the Anti-Lebanon mountains with
Mount Hermon brooding over the valley. The apartment was in
the uppermost part of the school and church compound built

into the hillside. Immediately below our balcony were the school playgrounds and the 140 steps to the road where we parked our newly bought car. Above the school and past the tethered donkey were our closest neighbours, their houses clinging to gravity-defying roads – narrow tracks of deeply scored concrete, poured to enable an eclectic assortment of vehicles access to the upper reaches of the town.

Spanking new SUVs swerved round donkeys laden with firewood and ancient cars which were kept on the road by the sheer willpower of their owners, and their frequent tinkering under the battered bonnets. The vehicles were a metaphor for the town. Many of the inhabitants struggled to make ends meet – houses were in desperate need of repair, rubbish clogged the streets, and the marks of the recent civil war were everywhere. But just round the corner new villas were going up, surrounded by huge walled enclosures, complete with the South American flags identifying the particular country where the family had made its money.

A microcosm of the town, our neighbourhood was mixed Sunni Muslim and Christian, middle income and poor. A walk to the souq via the precipitous back road would bring calls of *"Mayilu"* (come in and visit) from Mohammed and Hadije to their tiny three-room stone house, from Alia and her mother baking the flat mountain bread over the stick fire oven in what remained of their stables (mostly blown apart in the war), and from Abu Ali, the town's *mukhtar* (mayor) as he looked down from his shaded terrace, neatly framed with vines and kept scrupulously clean by the Sri Lankan family maid.

As in Jordan, we often accepted these invitations, and visiting our neighbours and being visited by them became a large part of our lives, particularly for Susanna. Once I started working at the school I had less time, and anyway the men were out at work during the day so it would have been inappropriate to visit. But for Susanna, the expectations were strong that she would spend hours going from home to home, drinking tea and chatting, getting to know the dramas of the neighbourhood, the events in the lives of the families around us. It involved gossip certainly, but also led to a powerful force of community cohesion. It was also an acute incentive to keep the house spotless, as a band of women might descend on the flat at any moment between the hours of eleven and two – and there was always the hidden agenda of checking up on how the foreigners were doing. A key measure here was how clean and tidy the house was.

My visits were rather different. For a start, they would mostly be in the late evenings. After work the men would go home, eat a late lunch and then sleep, emerging for the serious business of talking as the evening stars punctuated the shot-silk sky. In the summer, circles of plastic chairs were drawn up on the flat roofs of the houses, or on patios positioned to catch the evening breeze. In the winter, the same circles of men would cluster around the *soubia* (a wood or diesel-burning heater) in the centre of a formal lounge, complete with its Heath Robinson piping snaking the flue gasses out of a small hole in the wall.

Our discussion topics were different to the female conversations. Where the women talked of engagements, recipes, and children, we put the world to rights with heated debates centring on religion and politics. It was through listening, sharing, and questioning that I began to understand how these fathers, brothers, neighbours, and friends understood the world, how they lived with its inconsistencies, what they loved, what they hated – their stories. And, of course, they wanted to know about me. I was often grilled with rapid-fire questions, usually starting on safe ground. But, particularly if I was at Abdullah's house, these would quickly turn to deeper matters and so we learned about one another's worlds.

On an early visit, Abdullah had asked, "Why are you called Chris? What does it mean?"

"My parents liked the name. My full name is Christopher – like the saint who was supposed to have carried Christ over a river in Christian tradition."

"Charbel has a Saint Christopher on chain! So your father was called Chris?" Without waiting for a reply – it was an assumption rather than a question – he continued, "Do you know what my name means?"

I thought about it for a moment. Allah is the Arabic for God, used by both Christians and Muslims. It is closer to the biblical word (*El*) than the Germanic word (*Got*) that we use in English, but my mind was wandering. And *Abed* means servant or slave.

"Servant of God," I replied. "That's beautiful."

"I prefer Slave of God – that's strong!" And then Abdullah launched into a mini sermon. "I am proud to be called the slave of God. I want to submit to God – I want to obey him."

"I want to obey God too, but I also believe it is possible to love him. Jesus teaches that we can love God."

"Yes, yes, yes," continued Abdullah. "You Christians are always talking about Jesus. But for us, it is the Qur'an."

"Don't you mean Mohammed?"

"No! Mohammed (praise be unto him) is the great prophet, but you believe Jesus is the word of God, don't you?"

"Yes." I recited John chapter 1 verse 1: "In the beginning was the Word, and the Word was with God, and the Word was God."[9]

"Well," continued Abdullah, "it is the Qur'an that has always been with God. The Qur'an was in heaven coming to earth by revelation to Mohammed (praise be unto him); the Qur'an is the word of God!"

The power of Abdullah's words hit me. For the first time I understood the extraordinary veneration of the Qur'an in the lives of my Muslim friends and neighbours. The Qur'an is not the Muslim Bible – it is more like the person of Jesus Christ. No wonder it has to be treated with such respect. No wonder foolish Qur'anic burnings in the West enrage Muslim crowds.

Our introduction to the young people of the village was confusing. On an early return to the apartment, having paused

---

[9] NIV, UK 2011.

after the first 100 steps, Susanna was coaxing Sam and Chloe to complete the ascent. I struggled ahead, loaded down with the morning's groceries. From the flat roofs above us, mischievous laughter followed by sexualized swearing was spat at Susanna.

Shocked, I dropped the shopping and took chase. Horrified that the *ajaanib* (foreigner) responded as any of their neighbours would have done, the early teens scattered, leaping like goats down the urban terraces till they could join the street below, losing themselves in the anonymity of the souq. This was their domain and I had no chance of catching them but neighbours, drawn by the commotion, pointed helpfully in the direction of their flight and were happy to fill in the family details of the *miskalgies* (naughty boys). When I arrived in the road below, Abu Fouad was already waiting – the village telegraph having done its work. He knew what had happened, knew who the sinners were, and had a plan for justice.

He took me to Abu Musa, at his barbers' shop in the town square. This was the father of one of the boys. Some rapid-fire Arabic, gesticulating, pointing, tut-tutting and frequent "*ya harams*" (oh shame!) later and Abu Musa disappeared from the shop with a steely gaze and a determined step.

It wasn't long before he returned with the penitent Musa by the ear, trailed by his younger brothers and a gaggle of wide-eyed youths, eager to soak up the drama. Musa had clearly already received some of the justice Abu Fouad was keen to see, as evidenced by the welt on his glowing right cheek. Looking me straight in the eye, he made a fulsome apology. When he repeated the apology to Susanna, after the troupe made its way up to our house, he was deeply embarrassed – the picture of contrition – scrutinizing his sandalled feet throughout the ordeal.

My actions hadn't been carefully thought through or measured. They didn't come out of a missionary guidebook or "How would you respond in this situation?" seminar at Bible college. They were a gut response, impulsive. However, other than leaving Susanna with both kids and the shopping to carry up the last forty steps, they were right. We were beginning to respond instinctively in our new culture, and the preservation of Susanna's honour was paramount. Because the incident happened so early in our time in the village, it established at the outset to the *shabaab* (young men) that the foreigners weren't so different after all, and that the sexualized images beamed onto their TV sets and computers from Europe and North America did not represent all Western women.

Universally when we visited our neighbours their older children were impeccably polite. Girls as young as seven would serve us drinks. The boys, straight-backed, would sit in the formal guest lounge making polite conversation, talking about school, what they wanted to do when they grew up; subjects the world over when the generations meet. Older siblings would ensure the younger children's behaviour wasn't too riotous and, if their pampered early years were too much for the adult company, they would take them out or bribe them with sweets.

In the early months, we were always entertained in the formal sitting rooms of our neighbours' houses. These rooms were reserved for visitors, spotlessly clean, elaborately furnished, and decorated with the best the family could afford. For some this was reproduction Louis XVI furniture, complete with gilding, heavy curtains, crystal chandeliers, and faded French tapestries. For the less well-off, it was elaborate vases with artificial flowers on Formica coffee tables, and plastic chairs. These early visits were highly ritualized. After a formal greeting, which inevitably included an admonition for not visiting enough, we were seated, men on one side of the room, women on the other. Drinks appeared almost instantly with no one, seemingly, having left the room to prepare them, quickly followed by fruit or biscuits, cake, and tea. After chatting for half an hour or so, tiny cups of piping hot coffee, as black as a beetle's wing, would arrive with sugared almonds or individually wrapped chocolates in a crystal bowl or porcelain tray. This was the sign that we were free to leave, having performed our social obligations for a week or so.

As we got to know and become friends with the families around us, we were able to drop in more casually and, although we were always proffered sugary Arab sweetmeats, pastries and succulent fruit, we might sit in the family room, kitchen, or garden. Susanna had greater access behind the "family veil" than I did, as her relationships in the village were deeper and had passed from formality to the sharing of recipes in the kitchen, joint childminding, and the hopes and aspirations of the mothers for their children.

Whether the visits were formal or informal, on plastic or padded chairs, I was referred to as *Amo* (uncle) and Susanna as *Tante* (aunt) by the children, a familial formality that both respected the years between us and showed a comfort in relationships across the generations. The young people in the village were at ease with us because they were deeply comfortable with who they were. They were clearly, obviously, sometimes ostentatiously loved. Small children were the centre of attention. Toddlers and young children could do no wrong. There was an uncomfortable transition somewhere around seven years old when harsh reality hit (often literally), but as pre-teens they emerged confident and mature (in polite company at least).

It was in school that I had most of my exposure to the young people of the Bekaa, and after our brief introductory period of settling into the valley, Sam (aged five) and I had our first day at school; daunting for us both, in different ways. His first day at school anywhere would have been a big step (at least for us, his parents), but this was a huge school with over 3,000 students. It was into the primary department with its classes of over forty and virtually no spoken English that our brave, pale little boy, proudly wearing his light blue *maryul* (smock coat) strode. Susanna anxiously hung around the lower playground looking through the windows to see how he would settle.

He joined the class seated in a large ring on the floor. While the teacher seemed to be preparing the lesson, the children grew restless. Two boys were wrestling opposite Sam, so he got up, walked around the circle and clipped each round the ear – telling them in English to behave. Sam was going to be fine! Once the teacher emerged from her preparation she produced one green crayon, a large sheet of paper, and a cucumber. One by one the children came to the front and drew the vegetable in quick strokes on the soon-crowded piece of paper. Despite occasional exhortations from the teacher to "pay attention", the children, not being sure what they were supposed to pay attention to, carried on finding their own entertainment as they bickered and rolled around the floor, wrestling. Susanna, seeing Sam settled, if not being educated as we might have liked, left the playground thoughtfully.

With this as a start, we kept an eye on what Sam did in class – by way of work books sent home and my wandering down to the primary department when I had a free lesson. We were happy to see that although the work was not what one would describe as "child-centred" he was mostly kept busy with English and Arabic writing exercises, maths, colouring and reading.

On several occasions, the fact that his English was better than the teacher's would land him in trouble but, all credit to the school, they handled it diplomatically. Wrongly corrected when naming shapes, he insisted that the four-sided outline was a rectangle, not a square, all the way to the principal's office. The young teacher could not allow such open contradiction, but she wanted to know the precise English term and agreed that they would speak no more of it on return to the classroom. The naming of animals – an activity ubiquitous in primary classrooms – was trickier. The principal couldn't arbitrate between Sam and the teacher as to whether the picture in dispute was a lion or a tiger.

When so far out of one's culture, it is important not to draw conclusions too quickly. Sam's and our other children's education was a continuing source of concern, but the early lessons were not the full story. Although they all missed out on aspects of schooling typical of a British classroom, they learned other ways of looking at the world; new languages, the narratives of other nations and peoples, and geography not centred on Greenwich Mean Time. Perhaps above all they developed an identity in who they were, rather than one given to them by a system looking for conformity.

Not coming to conclusions too quickly was important for me too. Most of my first week was spent waiting in the staff room for something to do. I was here to head up the science department and take a lead in developing an exploratory, experimental approach to the subject. But the school administration did not believe I would come and then, when I did turn up, did not think I would be able to handle the discipline in the classroom. And the science faculty – they did not want an exploratory, let alone an experimental, approach, thanks very much!

This was not clear at the start. No one would tell me why I had nothing to do but slowly, as I gained trust with minor assignments, when the cover classes I taught did not end in riot, the situation clarified. A significant conversation with Ziad, who had taught in Canada and Lebanon, helped me make sense of the school's difficult position. He came into the staff room, empty except for me, and asked, "Don't you have a class?"

"No," I replied. "I wish I had, but no one is absent today so it is more Arabic grammar for me!" and I pointed to the language primer on the table.

"When you decided to come to live here, what did you think you would teach?"

"I had hoped to teach science and set up the lab; it hasn't been used in years. I also came to take chapels, and be available for the students in after-school clubs and at lunchtimes for activities and English practice."

"At least you are doing that. I heard your chapel talk yesterday – the kids were really listening when you spoke about how the worlds of science and religion don't contradict each other but are answering different questions. But I don't think you will ever get this science department to use the lab."

"Why not?"

"Because the science teachers see themselves as imparters of knowledge and, what's more, they have the most important knowledge in the school. They have it – they are paid to give it to the students. They will do that in the quickest, most efficient way, and the way that sticks in the minds of the kids, so they can pass their exams."

"But science is not just a collection of facts. It is an approach, a methodology, a powerful way of looking at the world – you develop an understanding as you use it, not as you memorize it."

Ziad pondered. "Yes, I agree – but that is not how we examine it, so it is not how we teach it. These kids need to pass the exams and they need knowledge, facts. Besides, class experiments take so much time to set up. It's so much easier to open a book and get the kids to learn it."

Shortly after this conversation, I had a meeting with the head teacher of the upper school. She bluntly stated that they had not thought I would be able to control the students but to her surprise, my cover classes had been quiet and orderly.

"You see," she explained "our school discipline is very different to school discipline in England or America. You have to be very tough, hard on the students. These kids will push you to the limit if you don't show them you are boss."

But finally it was agreed that I could teach a few classes: science to the lower years (where the general feeling was I would not do too much damage) and spoken English to the sixth form. However, the spoken English had to be in silence – otherwise they would get too rowdy and I would not cope.

I was delighted to be teaching my own lessons again. It wasn't easy. I refused to hit the students and would only expel the worst offenders from the classroom, where they waited in fear of the supervisors who patrolled the corridors. I only broke three wooden rulers on the desk in my efforts to get the classes to be quiet, but slowly my lessons became quieter and the students learned. In fact, "learned" was an important word to master for student and teacher alike. If I gave homework and casually said something like, "Read pages 3 to 5 and answer the questions on page 6", the immediate cry would come up, "Do you want us to study the pages or learn them?"

Initially puzzled, I soon realized this was the corollary of Ziad's teacher's perspective. To fully know the material from pages 3 to 5, the students felt they needed to memorize it. In that way any question on the material could be completed with the precise text. I was always careful to say *laazim tudrusu* (you must study) not *laazim tuhfuzu* (you must memorize).

Family life, divided between school and village, developed its own rhythm. It was an amalgam of what we brought with us: attitudes, behaviour patterns, British social norms, and the sometimes contradicting forces around us. Through neighbours, colleagues, shopkeepers and friends, new and very different ways of looking at the world were trickling in. Many came in quite naturally, often with the children from school, and were quickly absorbed. Others were so different that we needed to consider them carefully and decide what was acceptable and what was not. We mostly tried to develop one consistent code of behaviour, whether in or out of the house, but inconsistency was inevitable and was quickly picked up by the children. "But you said..." was the start of many conversations around the dinner table.

Food, eating times and the children's place at the family meals was one area where we quickly and easily adapted to the local norms. Breakfast, just as in England, was a hurried, chaotic affair. The eleven o'clock *mana'eesh* (a freshly baked bread base covered with olive oil, sesame, and sage) was enthusiastically added to our daily diet and meant that the late lunchtime of around three in the afternoon seemed quite reasonable, particularly as this was the end of the working day for me. Susanna and I tried to add an afternoon siesta to our timetable but our button-bright kids resisted it. There were always so many distractions, whether in the form of the donkey tethered to the back of the house, the new kittens born to the feral mother who looked little more than a kitten herself or, most commonly, the neighbourhood children, whose parents were most definitely going to sleep and so had sent the children to find their own entertainment at the house with so many toys.

With a late lunch, the evening meal would not be thought about till around seven, and with the preparation needed would not appear till eight or nine o'clock. In the village the whole family would eat this meal together, often with visitors, the children a key part in the daily social celebration. The youngest might be falling asleep over the *tabbouleh* but they received the message of inclusion with each mouthful. We found we could continue feeding Sam for a full five minutes after he had fallen asleep, when we were out particularly late with neighbours, his opening, chewing and swallowing continuing in reflex mode.

Like time, space was treated differently in the village. The first thing we noticed was how local attitudes diverged so widely between the treatment of privately owned and communal space. Without exception, our neighbours' homes were spotlessly clean, all the time. With huge pride, much of the morning was spent dusting, mopping, sweeping, and tidying so that the houses, whether grand or simple, were the picture of domestic hygiene. The men didn't help but they kept their cars equally pristine. We tried, but after the basic housework was complete, Susanna and I didn't have the heart to spend any more time polishing and, as for the car, the never-ending dust made cleaning pointless (at least, that was my excuse).

This was all in stark contrast to how we treated public space. Brought up with anti-litter campaigns and the great British sanctity of the countryside, we were physiologically incapable of dropping a sweet wrapper outside the house. Not so our neighbours. Two houses along from us, Um and Abu Fadi's house looked directly over a square of neglected weeds and rubble, the remains of an old village house destroyed in the civil war. The stone and adobe shell, shrinking with each winter rain, was filling up with rubbish. The family had the convenience of depositing their trash, neatly bundled in plastic bags, out of their lounge window into the waiting yard below. This saved them the trek to the dry stream bed where the rest of the neighbourhood dumped its rubbish.[10]

At school it was in the arena of "body space" that I noticed the greatest differences. As a Brit, I need more personal space than most. Trained in a culture that says "not too close", I felt uncomfortable if acquaintances leaned in towards me to make a point or, heaven forbid, poked my arm to check if I had understood. Here, I was in for a shock. On the first day the head of middle school needed to talk to me. He wanted to help me feel at home and give me some simple instructions. So he linked his arm in mine and we promenaded across the playground for ten minutes. I was acutely aware of the pupils around, thinking everyone would be looking at us. They didn't bat an eyelid, even when he changed tack and held my hand while looking me full in the face for another five long minutes.

Kissing was another difference. In England our stiff social etiquette is slowly changing and now it might be acceptable for one or two quick air kisses between the sexes, among friends. In Lebanon, the form is similar (although it is always three kisses to the cheeks), but that is where the similarity begins and ends. A mark of inclusion and friendship, men kiss men and women kiss women.

We discovered that children accept what is around them as normal in the most extraordinary ways. This became clear to us in the spring of our first year. We often heard the low rumble of conflict from the south as tensions waxed and waned across the Israeli-occupied strip of land around Marjayoun. In the April of 1996, however, these tensions boiled over as Israel launched an air assault aimed at ending rocket attacks into its northern territories. School was cancelled, refugees flooded into the town and we watched daily air strikes across the valley as supersonic jets destroyed targets in the hills of the Anti-Lebanon on the opposite

---

[10] When we arrived in the village there was no municipal rubbish collection. By the time we left Qab Elias, there was an efficient rubbish collection service.

side of the valley. Sam and Chloe's play changed. Alarmed, but glad the children could work through what was going on, we watched as they debated who was going to be the jet this time and who was going to get blown up. From then on, Chloe's favourite name for toys or imaginary playmates was "Bomb-John".

Refugees, fleeing the real-life destruction, squeezed into the houses of relatives up and down the steps from our house to the souq. Surprised to suddenly have an English family living alongside them, they were universally friendly and rather curious. Our neighbours had long since got used to us and were, in any event, used to foreigners living, on and off, in the apartment. These new arrivals reminded us of how different local and English forms of politeness can be. As we got to know these new families, we rehearsed the early stages of getting to understand a culture from the inside. Politeness, for example. If you judged local civility by your own norms of social etiquette you would be heading for trouble. At a meal table with friends in the village the words "Please" and "Thank you" would rarely be heard. Needed at an English meal to oil the conversation, here it would be semi-insulting to preface requests such as "Pass the salt" with "please", a word seen as highlighting formality, not friendship. Finishing all the food on the plate would, however, be terribly rude as it would give the impression that your host had not given you enough to eat. If you did need to say no, a flick of the head accompanied by a clicking of the tongue worked well, but you had to be careful not to admire an item in your host's living room or they would give it to you.

We learned and relearned these social graces, and all went smoothly until a trip back to England. Forgetting to warn the children of the different English protocol around food they would always leave food on their plates at the end of a meal and would indicate "No, I don't want to finish it", with a dismissive flick of the head to Grandma!

After nearly eighteen months of our new lives in the Bekaa, we were to be the recipients of special grace from friends, neighbours and colleagues as Susanna delivered our third child – Joshua – in hospital in the main town of Zahle. It had not been an easy pregnancy. Life with two small children at the top of 140 steps became more difficult as the bump got bigger. Over Christmas, temperatures plummeted and the early weeks of January saw deep falls of snow joining up the white peaks on either side of the valley.

After an emergency Caesarean, it was quickly clear all was not well and Josh was whisked away to intensive care. He had been born with pneumonia, which caused his fragile lungs to collapse after a few hours. The valley was all but cut off – the high pass taking the main road to Beirut buried in metres of snow. This meant that there would be no ambulance trip to the state-of-the art hospital in Beirut. Our tiny *zahlawi*, our precious baby and Zahle's newest resident, would fight for life in the incubator as the snow continued to fall over his home town.

The next two weeks were an exhausted blur. Susanna was discharged from hospital. Josh was left behind. We stayed with him alternately, supported by my parents who flew out to be with us from England, and our friends and neighbours. We were the targets of love – overwhelmed by grace from colleagues and friends. The birth of a baby is a huge celebration, but in the community the news was muted by the unspoken possibilities. Even while Susanna was still in hospital, she had a stream of visitors. Traditionally they should all be served with *mugli* (a mild milk pudding rather like baby food, covered with nuts). Our good friend and neighbour Hadije on her first visit discovered that we had no one serving our guests, so she took over, setting up a *mugli* station in the ward.

Slowly at first, but steadily, Josh improved. Although he could not travel to the hospital in Beirut he had an excellent pediatrician, recently returned from the US, in attendance. Under his attention and with the care of the nurses, our blue baby started to flush pink. His breathing strengthened and soon he was able to come off the ventilator. Tubes could be disconnected, and for the first time in a fortnight we were able to pick up and cuddle the newest member of the family. Bringing him home through the latest blizzard was nerve-wracking as he had only known the heat of the intensive care unit but he seemed unfazed and quickly adjusted to the rather different surroundings of home, with two very inquisitive siblings and a seemingly never-ending stream of visitors giving us their congratulations, blessings, and love.

CHAPTER 4

A History Told in Stone

1997
Baalbek, Byblos, Beirut, Tyre, Anjar, Lebanon

We were standing on the largest cut stone anywhere on the planet. As big as two squash courts and weighing in at a colossal 1,500 tons, it easily beats other building block heavyweights, and it was carved nearly 2,000 years ago by the Romans. We were at Baalbek, the most extraordinary complex of ancient buildings in the northern Bekaa. A collection of superlatives, it contained the largest Roman temple ever built and has the most complete Roman temple standing. It was also our favourite afternoon outing for those times when the kids really needed to get out of the apartment, to run around and climb.

Unusually, the ruins were full. We were making use of the *Eid el Fitr* holiday, along with other families, enjoying the majestic open spaces. Marvelled at by tourists and studied by amateur and professional historians alike, the local townsfolk promenaded the wide Roman streets with their magnificent classical backdrop. Following the recent air campaign by Israel, regional tensions were high and so internationals were thin on the ground, which meant we often had these antique wonders to ourselves. But not today. Today they were buzzing. Extended families, young couples, gaggles of girls and posses of boys thronged the boulevards, or posed for photos, Lilliputian-like, at the base of one of the six remaining, unbelievably vast, pillars of Jupiter's temple.

We had followed our usual route: haggling at the ticket office for a local entrance fee, we joined the family in their holiday best making their way up the grand entrance steps, past the pink Egyptian granite columns, and into the first courtyard. This was where the children could run. With an eagle eye on the older two, we dodged the flirting couples and sped round the Roman circus of the unique hexagonal precinct and on into the expanse of the Great Court. Insisting on holding hands, we climbed the central altar with its dizzying unprotected drops. But walking up the processional steps to the Temple of Jupiter, you couldn't rush. Climbing the steep steps, a sense of awe would descend, slowing, silencing the crowd until you emerged with a collective gasp at what remained after two millennia. On everybody's mind – what would it have looked like in Roman times?

In something of a daze, we gingerly shepherded the kids to the pillars, set on a man-made promontory, like a cliff overlooking the smaller, near-complete Temple of Bacchus. Earthquakes had knocked a few pillars askew but, near perfect, it sits like a David Roberts lithograph framed by the snow-capped peaks of Mount Lebanon to the west. Always a favourite with the kids, we were on our way down to find Medusa, turned to stone in myth and here in reality adorning one of the limestone slabs dislodged from the ceiling. We paused to let a brightly coloured flock of teenage girls descend the narrow and rickety wooden stairway, their calls of delight and mock fear echoing around the human-made canyon. Here we were targeted. We stood out. We were the only foreigners around, and so marked.

He came up to us with two black plastic bags, beckoning that we follow; speaking in English, he said he had treasure. His attitude was different to the souvenir touts at the entrance, less demanding and more sure that what he had we would want to see, and what we saw, we would want to buy. I followed him into an alcove, little more than a niche, its ceiling the inner curve of a marine shell, sea nymphs and dolphins cavorting in the calcified waves on the stone blocks obscuring the entrance. Sure enough, he had treasure. Sam had heard the conversation; his seven-year-old dreams were coming true. We just needed Indiana Jones to complete the scene. The first artefact out of the bag was a miniature bronze of a god with winged feet. Lithe, liquid in its grace, the ebony patina glistened in the sun.

"You like?" the antique dealer enquired.

"He's Hermes," piped up Chloe, who was elbowing her way past her older brother to get a better look.

"*Shaatra* – she is clever. Would you like to hold him?"

Realizing we would soon have the children playing with priceless antiquities, I needed to regain some control.

"Yes, she knows all the Roman and Greek legends. But where did you get it from and why are you selling them? This should be in a museum."

"If you think this one should be in a museum, what about this?" he asked, all the time unwrapping a second package. As the plastic fell away, a seated figure of anemic alabaster stared out at us blindly, coal-black eyes vacant.

"This is very old, Babylonian."

"Where did you get it?" I asked, knowing how privileged we were to see and touch something so beautiful, so old, and so valuable.

"I know a place," he mumbled.

Before I could stop him, he emptied coins into the children's outstretched, upturned hands. Silver Roman emperors, bronze eagles and a golden laurel wreath made the children's fingers seem particularly small. Whether the artefacts were real or not I could not be sure, but the coins certainly excited the kids. Treasure indeed. Having carefully counted the coins back into his bag we retreated, joining a gaggle of schoolchildren who were noisily making their way to the second temple. On returning to the village, I asked a neighbour and friend who taught history at the local school,

"Would the objects have been real or fake?" He couldn't be sure. Most likely fakes, he thought, but if you scratched the Bekaa, you dug deep into human history. Many of the archaeological sites, ancient mounds mostly, were raided through the years of civil war and even today an unscrupulous tomb robber with a metal detector could steal the treasure of a nation while trashing the clues to any historical importance.

With work, church, neighbourhood obligations, two children at school and a new baby, we were pretty busy. Nevertheless, during our years in the Bekaa we found that the children had both long summer breaks and frequent religious holidays that, thanks to the non-alignment of the Islamic and Gregorian calendars, were randomly scattered through the academic terms. Add to this the dawning realization that their English curriculum required supplementing, we needed a plan if the children were to benefit from the cultural richness around them.

Our solution was to keep them busy and teach them English by studying local history. It started as a collection of family outings, spurred on by our trip to Baalbek, but developed into an extended home school project, with research at the historical sites and a write-up by way of an enormous timeline that we stuck to the walls, snaking its way through the house. When you live in the Bekaa your local history soon becomes global, as most civilizations seemed to have passed through at one stage or another.

Our first date on the timeline came from the stony shore of Lake Qaraoun, in the south of the valley. Bordered by olive groves sloping down to the reservoir, the site first recommended itself as an ideal picnic spot. The trees, hunched and squat like old women with firewood on their backs, leaned at precarious angles. The black of their trunks contrasted with the riot of colour around their roots – claret-red cyclamen in the deepest shade, trailing to pink, and then the communion white of Egyptian Honesty glistening in the sun. The marshmallow colour scheme hid a miniature garden. Bright orange tulips emerged from leaves pinched like a pie crust, a host of orchids mimicked the iridescent bodies of flies and wasps, and the smoky blue tassels of hyacinths tossed in the breeze.

There was plenty for a family to explore here, beauty and sun for Susanna to soak up, a mini beast safari for Dad and the older kids, and stones for toddler Josh to throw into the water; except some of those stones were rather oddly shaped. Beautifully smoothed and crafted, the one Josh had been about to throw fitted perfectly into the palm of my right hand. It had a notch for my thumb as four fingers comfortably held the dulled blade that had not seen use for over 10,000 years. The mini beast safari forgotten, further exploration came up with an arrow head, a couple of small hand axes and a thin scraper, all made from flint between 12,000 and 10,000 BC. This had been a Neolithic camp and was part of the largest collection of Stone Age tools anywhere in the world; scattered in the southern Bckaa and bearing testimony to just how long this valley had been inhabited. So, at home, we marked the bathroom door at the far end of the hall with "12,000 BC" and covered the corridor walls up to the boys' bedroom with photos of the flints and imaginative dioramas painted by the children.

For the start of recorded history, we needed a trip to the oldest city in the region and perhaps the world: Byblos. Even its name plays leapfrog with the millennia. Today the road signs, as you leave the autostrade, declare it to be Jbail, the Arabic form of the Bronze Age Gubal, but it is better known to the world by its ancient Greek name, Byblos, which gives us the word "Bible". In crusader times it was Gibelet, and it is the twelfth-century castle that first greets you at the World Heritage Site, sprawling its way down to the ancient harbour, still port to the local fishing boats.

With three small children, we were always early whenever we set off for a family outing. Bleary-eyed but missing the worst of the Beirut traffic, we arrived at the town for an early lunch after our trek across the mountains to Beirut and then north up the coastal highway. The narrow coastal strip, unlike the Bekaa, was densely populated, and even when finally out of Beirut the once-separate towns were continuous with ugly ribbon development. After an hour of bumper-to-bumper driving, high rise blocks gave way to banana plantations, with great scoops taken for roadside diners. From the dawn of civilization this narrow fertile strip, bordered by the Mediterranean Sea to the west and the Mount Lebanon range to the east, had been an important centre of population. With the bounty of the sea a fish hook away, an idyllic climate and light soils irrigated by mountain-fed springs, small wonder this was one of the ancient world's most desirable postcodes.

The whole town was historic. Dig a hole and you would bring up Roman pottery or Greek amphorae, but the magnet drawing the visitors was the excavated site from the castle to the sea. With our intrepid, miniature students of history, we hurtled around the keep. Alarming sheer drops without handrails quickened the pulse of us parents while human skulls and bone fragments poking from massive stone sarcophagi excited the kids. We could have filled our entire timeline from this one site, as Neolithic implements found in the lowest strata gave way to coins of the twentieth- century French mandate in the museum, with everything in between.

Chasing round the labyrinth of paths we travelled helter-skelter through the ages. Guarded by impossibly thick stone walls nearly 5,000 years old, the children played hide and seek behind Greek columns, recited nursery rhymes on a perfect miniature Roman stage complete with its tiered stone seats, and marvelled at the obelisks raised to Baal, the idol they had been reading about in their Old Testament Bible stories.

We had plenty of source material for the next several patches of wall. The Bronze Age dawned around 3300 BC and was marked on our timeline by photos of the massive walls we marvelled at. Trade began with Egypt and Mesopotamia, the other centres of early human civilization in the Fertile Crescent, mapped in every primary school history text. Byblos grew and became the most important port and trading centre on the coast. The earliest Lebanese export was cedar wood, and on their return journeys trading ships would have brought back alabaster, gold, linen, and papyrus. Relations were not always commercial, however. From 1530 to 1271 BC, first the Egyptians, then the Hittites and then the Egyptians again flexed their military muscles as they absorbed the coastal city states such as Byblos into their empires.

Just a little further along our corridor we marked the invasion of the Sea Peoples in 1200 BC and the succeeding centuries as the "Phoenician Golden Age". These were a remarkable people, taking over the city states along the coast, Byblos included. Great navigators, they founded outposts as far from their home shores as Carthage in modern-day Tunisia and on to the Spanish coast. Famed in the ancient Near East for their trade in purple – the dye made from murex seashells – they are better known today as inventors of the alphabet. Egyptian hieroglyphs and Assyrian cuneiform were unsuitable for the needs of these early businessmen. The Phoenician traders had to keep track of cargo loads and destinations, profits and loss. Their breakthrough was to develop a phonetic script that represented sounds, and the economy with which they achieved this is preserved in the family of alphabets descended from this revolutionary idea, including the one you are reading.

Persians followed Babylonians who, in their turn, lost an empire to the Greeks under the extraordinary figure of Alexander the Great. A pawn in the clash of the powerbrokers of the time, the Phoenician cities mostly welcomed Persia's defeat by Alexander. For the next 300 years, Hellenization moulded the culture in architecture, sculpture, fashion, and religion. One city did try to hold out against Alexander in a siege that lasted seven months and, as we discovered when we visited, the result of his victory can still be seen in the landscape. Sur, or Tyre as it is known in English, used to be built on an offshore island, the citizens confident of their natural defences. Alexander's answer was to build a causeway using tons of rocks and thousands of tree trunks. The city was defeated and the causeway with its extraordinary story made its way onto our wall at 333 BC, just short of Chloe's bedroom door, as Old Tyre is built on the promontory to this day.

We had plenty of material for the Roman period. Quite when this started is complicated – so we added dashes to our timeline, now a dado rail around Chloe's bedroom. The Romans increased in influence with the defeat of their rival power in the Mediterranean – the Phoenician colony of Carthage in 201 BC. The entire region, in the form of the province of Syria, was annexed by Pompey the Great, the adversary of Julius Caesar in the Roman Civil war, in 64 BC. Chloe's bedroom walls were decorated with Latin numerals, mosaic pictures and, of course, Chloe's favourite, the pantheon of the gods – identified with their Roman and Greek names. It wasn't just from Baalbek that we drew inspiration. Seemingly every Lebanese town and village had a Roman ruin, with a fair scattering in the countryside romantically isolated from the modern, often mundane, architecture of the towns. Particular family favourites were the upper temple of Niha, nestled in the almond and cherry orchards in the lower folds of Mount Sannine, and the tiny ruin at Ain Hourche, one of the cluster of temples that ring Mount Hermon, far off the beaten track.

Now our timeline was entering the New Testament era and so we marked Jesus' visits to Tyre and Sidon (Matthew 15:21) and Paul's missionary journeys. It was always a theory of ours that Saul met the risen Christ on the Damascus highway at the pass of Daher el Baida, overlooking the Bekaa. The modern mountain motorway with its switchbacks and rally-style driving is certainly a place where many travellers have met their Maker in recent years. There is also a widely held view that the Mount of Transfiguration may have been Mount Hermon. It is certainly the highest peak in the area where the Gospels put Christ immediately prior to his climb with Peter, James, and John (Matthew 16 and 17).

With Constantine's conversion to Christianity in AD 330 the Roman world was gradually Christianized. Giving momentum to a conversion starting in the east, it eventually became the state religion in AD 380 with the Emperor Theodosius. Churches were built, many temples destroyed; others were converted for use by the new religion. The best-known example of this ancient form of recycling is the Temple of Jupiter in Damascus which became the Cathedral of John the Baptist and is now the Great Mosque. After the death of Theodosius, the Roman Empire split into the Western and Eastern or Byzantine Empire. Of the two, only the Byzantine Empire lasted. Rome was sacked in AD 410 but Byzantium remained the capital of lands that waxed and waned until 1453 with the arrival of the Ottoman Turks and its capture.

In contrast to much of Europe, the Near East enjoyed a period of prosperity and security. Enriched by the Silk Route, spices, silk thread and cloth from China graced the markets of Alexandria and Beirut. Largely Christian, it was in this Eastern Empire that ideas and images of the faith were expressed in the literary languages of the various regions[11] laying the foundations of the Orthodox traditions: Greek, Armenian, Syriac, and Copt. Emerging from Chloe's room, the timeline rejoined the corridor, decorated by Eastern crosses.

By the sixth century, the Byzantine Empire all but surrounded the Mediterranean Sea, from the Straits of Gibraltar to the Levant, Egypt, and the North African littoral to the south, and Greece in the north. Neighbouring this antique empire lay a very different landscape, beyond the Red Sea. The oases of the deserts of the Arabian Peninsula were peopled by tribes of settled cultivators. There were craftsmen and traders in small market towns and Bedouin nomads moving with their camels, sheep, and goats between the ephemeral pastures of the steppe. There had long been interchange between the Arabic-speaking desert dwellers and their northern neighbours. Arab pastoral nomads were settled in the interior of Syria and lower Iraq and Jewish craftsmen and merchants and Christian monks lived in the oases of the Hijaz.[12]

---

[11] A. Hourani, *A History of the Arab Peoples*, London: Faber & Faber, p. 8.

[12] Hourani, *A History of the Arab Peoples*, p. 12.

To the east, the Sassanid civilization were the great rivals. A constant thorn in the Byzantine side they had been at war, on and off, for centuries. Both sides, spent by conflict and decimated by disease, had their last accounting in AD 629 when the Byzantines finally took back Mesopotamia and Syria. In Arabia it was different – a young, vibrant vision was taking hold. The historian Albert Hourani, quoting contemporary writers, talks of: "a world waiting for a guide and a man searching for a vocation"[13] That guide was Mohammed, and to explore the consequences of that vocation, we set off across the Bekaa to a town called Anjar – where the archaeological site preserves in stone the meeting of the three civilizations.

Ironically, the modern town of Anjar is an Armenian community, part of a nineteenth-century forced migration of the Ottoman era, but the ruins alongside the neat tree-lined streets are of an important early Islamic site founded at the dawn of the eighth century. We parked outside the entrance hut in the shade of a plane tree, against the heat that would build through the day and make the steering wheel of the car impossible to touch by the time we got back. The noise of the family disembarking from the car woke the *natur*, the guardian of the site, who had been dozing to the sound of cicadas. He issued us tickets and told us not to interfere with the archaeologists working inside.

First thing on the agenda for the kids was to run. The wide grassy bridleways built for the caravans pausing on their journeys along the road linking Beirut with Damascus were ideal. Lining the narrower streets in a different quarter of the ruins, the remains of some 600 shops bore testimony to the commercial importance of the site, and they proved an ideal backdrop for the children to recreate an ancient shopping experience. It was here that we met the German archaeological team, the only other visitors sharing the arcades with us, with their magnificent views of the still snow-capped peaks of Mount Lebanon framed by graceful two-tiered

---

[13] Hourani, *A History of the Arab Peoples*, p. 15.

arches. Turning into a passageway off the main square, itself marked by the remnants of a cubic Roman monument, we met Ingrid, one of the German scholars, lifting up and peering under the stones that lined the route.

"What are you doing?" enquired Sam.

"Taking photos," she replied. "You see the Arabic inscriptions on the undersides of these carved stones?" She lifted the block higher so we could all see. "I am making a record of them." She got down to the level of the children. "They are really important – like this place. The carving on this stone could be Byzantine. Look at the Roman motifs – but on the other side it is Arabic Script. It is just like the site – there is a Roman bathhouse and a mosque! The columns look Byzantine but they were laid out by Islamic town planners. This place comes from a time when the world changed. The Arab tribes that united under the new religion of Islam took over huge stretches of land, defeating the weakened Byzantines within a generation of the Prophet's vision of a universal religion."

The first centre of administration and power was just up the road from Anjar, in Damascus under the Umayyad Caliphate. After only ninety years, it moved to the newly built Baghdad as the Abbasid dynasty took over. This was longer lasting, and it was not till AD 969 that the Fatimids seized power and the centre of the Islamic world moved to the new city in the region – Cairo. By AD 750, just 120 years after the death of Mohammed, the Islamic caliph controlled an area from the shores of the Atlantic in modern-day Spain and Portugal, to the Indus River in what today we call Pakistan. With a stable and highly efficient bureaucracy and government, there was an unparalleled flourishing of the arts and sciences. Here lived the medieval giants of medicine, astronomy, navigation, town planning, philosophy, natural history, poetry, and much more besides. The following cameos of some of the most important men of the period made it onto our timeline, filling the space between Chloe's and the boys' bedroom doors.

Al-Razi (865–925) was born in Rey, in modern-day Iran. A polymath, he is best known for his contribution to medicine. He differentiated, for the first time, measles and smallpox. Directing a large hospital in Baghdad, he pioneered the practice of taking detailed case histories and clinical notes, and his writings formed the basis of standard medical texts for Islamic and European medical students for centuries.[14]

Ibn Sina (known as Avicenna in the West) (980–1037) was born in Afshana near Bukhara in Central Asia. He was another physician but is better known as a philosopher who had a decisive impact on Thomas Aquinas among others, through his writings on self-existence and the soul.[15]

Ibn Khaldun (1332–1406) was born in Tunisia and worked in Morocco, Spain, and Egypt. He is remembered for his attempts to unify the subjects of politics, economics, philosophy, and most particularly, history.[16] A polymath in the great tradition, he even foreshadowed Darwin in this extraordinary passage from his magnum opus the Muqaddimah:

One should then look at the world of creation. It started out from the minerals and progressed, in an ingenious, gradual manner, to plants and animals. The last stage of minerals is connected with the first stage of plants, such as herbs and seedless plants. The last stage of plants, such as palms and vines, is connected with the first stage of animals, such as snails and shellfish which have only the power of touch. The word "connection" with regard to these created things means that the last stage of each group is fully prepared to become the first stage of the next group.[17]

---

[14] www.sciencemuseum.org.uk/broughttolife/people/alrazi.aspx (accessed 4.11.14).
[15] www.iep.utm.edu/avicenna/ (accessed 4.11.14).
[16] www.muslimphilosophy.com/ik/klf.htm (accessed 4.11.14).
[17] http://asadullahali.files.wordpress.com/2012/10/ibn_khaldun-al_muqaddimah.pdf (accessed 11.11.14). Abd Ar Rahman bun Muhammad ibn Khaldun, *The Muqaddimah*, trans. Franz Rosenthal, pp. 137–38.

Ibn Battuta (1304–69), born in Tangiers, was the greatest explorer of the age. His travels of some 75,000 miles took him to West and East Africa, making it as far as Mombasa on the coast, through Arabia and the Near East to Central Asia, Persia, and India. Continuing by way of Ceylon, he explored South East Asia as far as Sumatra and north into China.

We lived about 120 miles from Jerusalem and only 70 miles from the Sea of Galilee. A migrating stork could be spiralling on a thermal of hot air above the Dome of the Rock at breakfast and over our house by coffee break. But the modern-day political realities of the Middle East meant that the Holy Land was inaccessible, the Israel–Lebanon border closed to all, except the birds. The same was true in the eleventh century, when European pilgrims were blocked from what they saw as the holiest city in the world, the very centre of their universe. This was an unusual state of affairs, as up until this time the Muslim authorities had granted passage and hospitality to the Christian travellers. Relations between the Byzantine Church and the papacy on one side and the Islamic Caliphate on the other were increasingly hostile but spiralled down to new lows as the Pope preached a sermon calling knights to arms for the First Crusade.

In all, there were eight crusades over a period of two centuries. In the short term the Frankish knights were successful in their objective; capturing Jerusalem and massacring thousands of its inhabitants in 1099. They founded kingdoms and held court far from home. Their greatest legacies in stone, however, reflect their reception by the people of the region – fortified castles. The largest castle in the world is the crusader fortification of Crac de Chevaliers in modern-day Syria. On a short holiday one Easter, we visited the site, complete with moat, drawbridge, outer walls and keep, like a Norman castle back home but on a colossal scale. Built to withstand a siege, the castles, like the tiny kingdoms, were in a perpetual state of war, sometimes even among themselves. In decline from 1187 when they suffered heavy losses at the hand of Salah ad Din at the Battle of Hattine, the last crusaders were finally driven out in 1291 by the Mamelukes, successors to the dynasty founded by the legendary Muslim ruler.

The crusader castles, European transplants, are fascinating places to visit. The most extraordinary of them all for us didn't make it onto our timeline as it was off-limits when we were home-schooling the kids. But in May 2000, the Israeli army withdrew from the occupied zone in the far south of Lebanon, opening up the hitherto inaccessible Beaufort Castle. We followed the streams of mostly Shiite refugees as they poured back into their home villages. In the first few days after the military evacuation, curious foreigners as well as locals could see for themselves a part of their country that although just down the road, might as well have been on a different continent until the Israelis withdrew.

The castle itself sits high above the Litani River Valley with magnificent views across the hills of southern Lebanon and on into northern Israel. We had been warned by the local news reports that wandering off well-worn tracks was not recommended. Unexploded ordnance had already claimed the lives of several adventurous tourists, but we were still surprised to have to park the car next to a minefield to join the crowds of flag-waving Lebanese scampering over the ruins. As we ascended the crumbling peak the castle seemed to grow from the rock itself. With a desolate bleached beauty it completed the hillside, seemingly a natural extension of the limestone bedding planes, only given away by the occasional handrails and clumsy modern lookout on the tower. As Colin Thubron says of a similar site: "ruin has lent it a chance perfection, what was once heavy and corrupt is now slenderness and grace: a temple for a shepherd".[18] Not so the recent additions around the keep; ugly concrete bunkers, abandoned gunmetal-grey tools of war, and over all the exultant green and yellow flags of Hezbollah whipping in the wind.

The next great empire on the block was the Ottomans. Having finally taken the city of Byzantium in 1453, they ruled the region

---

[18] Colin Thubron, *The Hills of Adonis*, London: Penguin, 1987, New York, NY: Vintage, 2008, p. 181.

for an extraordinary 400 years, only losing control with their defeat at the end of the First World War. Field trips to the Ottoman splendour of downtown Beirut changed greatly over our years in Lebanon. In the early days during a visit to central Beirut, the children would count the "tea bag buildings" so full of holes it was a wonder they stayed standing. But slowly the government restored great sections of the territory so fiercely fought over during the civil war years, reclaiming their Ottoman grandeur. Graceful arcaded walkways, intricate ironworked balconies, high-end boutiques and smart cafés filled the restored streets, giving a honey stone façade to the chaotically authentic working neighbourhoods behind.

To understand the fate of the region post-Second World War, we watched the 1962 epic *Lawrence of Arabia*. In the devastating simple lines delivered by General Allenby's aide, the next period in the life of Lebanon and the region are mapped out:

> *Mr Sykes is an English civil servant; Mr Picot is a French civil servant. Mr Sykes and Mr Picot met and they agreed that after the war France and England should share the Turkish Empire, including Arabia. They signed an agreement ... to that effect.*

In Lebanon the French mandate lasted till 1943. At independence there was an agreement between the Christian president Bechara el Khoury and his Sunni Muslim ally Riad el Solh, known as the National Pact. Never written down, it defined Lebanon as an independent country with an "Arabic aspect", apportioning government positions to the major confessions: a Maronite Christian president, a Sunni Muslim prime minister and a Shiite speaker of parliament.

We decided that independence was a good place to end the timeline, partly as we had run out of wall, but mostly because our quiet summer schools were increasingly interrupted by history working itself out on the street – but more of that in later chapters.

CHAPTER 5

Grounded in the Valley

1996–98
The Bekaa Valley, Lebanon

It was nearly Christmas. Leaden skies locked the valley shut, draining all colour from the hills. Thin columns of grey smoke coiled, twisting vertically from every house, as the diesel stoves brought warmth to the *uddit ishitte* (winter room), the one room in every home that was kept heated and where family life congregated, in defiance of the cold outside. I had just come back into our own winter room after shovelling the snow off the flat roof. If it accumulated, it would slowly melt from the heat of the house, and drip through the ceilings, adding to the dank chill. Our Christmas tree was decorated and carols were playing but Susanna's and my mood matched the weather – depressed. Christmas can be a hard time to be away from home and Lebanon was not yet home. We needed to do something – we needed to form our own family traditions. We decided that part of that would be to attend the English carol service at the Anglican church in Beirut.

We normally avoided the highway linking the Bekaa with Beirut in the winter. With the pass at 2,000 metres, it was easy to get stuck on the wrong side as the road would frequently close with drifting snow. The forecast promised better weather, however, for the coming Sunday, and anyway, the thought of getting stuck in Beirut was currently quite appealing.

The Sunday before Christmas dawned bright and clear. The excited children, wrapped up against the biting wind, dived into the back of the car as we loaded our bright red and blue plastic sledges into the boot along with snow chains for the tyres, thermoses filled with tea, boots galore, a picnic lunch and enough coats and scarves to kit out a kindergarten. We decided to make the best of the snow that remained on the higher slopes en route, planning to arrive in Beirut for a late lunch and then on to the evening carol service.

As we turned west onto the sweeping intersection of the Damascus highway, at the foot of the mountain, we joined the buses, cars, and lorries jostling for a slot in the caravan snaking its way up the hill, each trying to avoid the icy verge on one side and the oncoming traffic screaming down the hill on the other. Occasionally the road would gridlock as cars, two or three abreast, overtook heavy-laden lorries crawling uphill, only to meet the same lane overspill on the way down. But steadily we climbed, past the drive-in snack bars, petrol stations and oily garage forecourts, to the open snowfields, virgin white, sullied only at their edges by the black corruption from the road.

Just before the pass, we turned off the motorway and gingerly drove a few hundred metres to a clearing in the snow, overlooking a slope seemingly made for sledging. Grateful for the near-perfect conditions, we were a little puzzled as to why the parking had been cleared but no other families chose this spot. Others seemed to prefer to park on the highway itself, making quick forays into the snow to build snowmen on the bonnets of their cars – proof, when they returned to Beirut, of their snowy adventure. But soon, whizzing down the hillside, looking like it was covered in fondant icing, we discovered why we were alone in this winter wonderland – or rather that we were not alone, as we were soon speeding through the outlying tents of a Syrian army camp.

The Syrian army had been occupying Lebanon since the end of the civil war and was well entrenched at all levels of the politics and administration of the country, as well as the landscape. In common with our Lebanese neighbours, we avoided the camps as much as possible. Relations between the soldiers and the locals were often strained, and there were rumours of murders on both sides. But now the family was careering in bright plastic sledges past Russian-made tanks, half-submerged in the snow. In a spray of ice crystals the sledges spun to a stop as we used our feet as brakes.

Hastily buttoning up their trench coats, a small group of soldiers ran towards us. They had been warming their hands over a fire in an old oil barrel when we shot past them, catapulting them from their frozen doze into action.

"Stop! Who are you? What are you doing here?" barked the least dishevelled and so presumably superior officer.

"Sorry, we didn't know there was army here – we are just playing in the snow with our children," I replied.

At this point, Chloe gave a beatific smile to the assembled khaki-clad crowd, which was swelling with each passing second.

"*Habibi!*" the corporal crooned.

We knew we were going to be fine. After a scolding for not better protecting our kids (he had a point), we were pulled back up the hill by eager volunteers, the children sucking on the boiled sweets proffered by the conscripts.

After the excitement of the morning, the carol service was a calm delight. It was restoring to sing the familiar songs and perform the comforting seasonal rituals, spiced up by the international crowd. After the service we were invited back for supper to the home of Chris and Alison Walley at the American University of Beirut. On something of an emotional high, fuelled by using so much English, we sat and chatted after the meal as our kids explored the foreign delights of a children's play park with its exotic furniture of swings and slides.

Discovering that we lived in the West Bekaa and that I was a keen birdwatcher, Chris told us about the efforts he was involved in, through the university, to support the new government programme establishing protected areas in the country – sanctuaries from the headlong rush for development and the ubiquitous hunting. Within the scientific community, largely based in the capital, there was a widely held belief that one of the candidates for protection had been irretrievably damaged through the war years and so unlikely to make the grade for the new protected area programme. After poring over a map we realized it was the wetland that we had visited in our first days in the valley. For the first time we heard the name Aammiq, a name and a place that would reshape our work and lives in ways we couldn't begin to imagine. I promised to return to the wetland to check out whether it was still used by migrating birds.

It was mid-February before I was able to make good my promise to birdwatch at the marsh. The winter had been long, cold, and wet and work in the school and village had kept Susanna and I busy since Christmas. But a free Saturday afternoon with the first promise of spring warmth turned my thoughts to what the marsh might hold. I drove south, past the quarries which pockmarked the hillsides and covered the poorest of the villages in a white, leprous dust. Suddenly I burst into beauty with a bend in the road. Finally leaving the urban sprawl behind, the gracious curve of Mount Lebanon cradled the emerald green of the West Bekaa, and at its heart was Aammiq. The majesty of the mountain seemed to come down lower here, its wildness seeping onto the plain with the spring water flooding the seasonal marshes. The road was an asphalt interruption in the Holm Oak forest's march downhill.

I parked in the lengthening shadows of *Qala'et el Mudiq*, a contorted hill of buckled bedding planes thrust up from geological depths, which forced the road to dog-leg eastwards. Here in the late afternoon sun, the reed beds glowed with inner warmth contrasting with the coldness of the crystal-clear water emerging in deep pools from the roots of the mountain. Goat tracks criss-crossed the palette of green and grey as a low grass sward filled the spaces between the rain-sculptured rocks, only the thick waxy leaves of the ground-hugging *ornithogalums* with their white six-pointed star of Bethlehem flowers surviving the voracious appetites of the grazers.

Looking east it was easy to see why some in the conservation community questioned whether enough wildlife had survived the war years to make this a contender for protection. Wide drainage ditches scoured deep into the fields hemming in the reed beds and pools of open water. Great pumps were standing ready for drier times when the same fields would rob the wetland of its water through irrigation instead of drainage. The lowest branches of the willow trees, pendulous above the receding ponds, were festooned with garbage – having sampled the run-off waste at the height of the flood. Empty plastic sacks, with their stark warnings of potent pesticides, hinted at the unseen alchemy leaching through the landscape. The same water that fed or poisoned the wetland provided for the needs of the Bedouin community, their stitched sacking tents crowded on one of the few remaining meadows not taken by the plough. Some thirty or so families were living a few inches proud of the high-water mark, clear of the decaying mats of algae, carcasses of dead fish, and bleached plastic bottles.

From the evenly spaced figures bending in lines along the furrows of the adjacent field, it was clear that the nomads were working as farm labourers, planting beet or maize in the drying mud that only a few years ago would have had a natural crop of Reedmace, pond weed, or sedge. As I watched, a trailer pulled by an ancient tractor stopped to disgorge its human cargo. A party of young Bedouin women, raucous and merrily dressed, each topped with a conical straw hat, ended their working day in the fields to begin the domestic chores around the campsite. Collecting large aluminium pails, half a dozen went to draw water for cooking while others began the task of washing clothes, pots and pans in the pools behind the camp. Next to the largest of the tents a simple stockade had been built of thorny bushes, taken from the hill on the other side of the road, and it was here that the last of the girls was headed. Completing the biblical scene, the sheep were waiting and passive as they were corralled and tethered forming a line, heads interlocking, enabling the now milkmaids easy milking.

I hadn't seen any men in the camp but they had seen me and it wasn't long before a couple of gangly youths approached to invite me to their father's tent for coffee. With the thought of coffee, I suddenly realized that I was getting cold. The long shadow of the western hills was already marching across the valley, the sun having slipped behind the ridge some minutes before.

The tent was dark but warm inside, a simple wood stove providing a flickering light. The bitter, piping-hot coffee was in an elaborate brass pot. Abu Nizar was the proud father of three boys and four girls. Most of the year they lived in Homs in Syria but each spring, and sometimes in the autumn, they would get the tent out of storage and make the trek to the Bekaa for extra work. He had only brought his five younger children with him this year. Nizar, his eldest son, was studying engineering at university in Syria, and his younger brother was doing compulsory military service. Abu Nizar was not sure where – perhaps here in Lebanon.

We talked about the wetland. The family loved coming here in the spring. The work was good but they also loved the clean fresh air, the mountains and the luxuriant grass for their flock, but they did not like coming in the autumn. Abu Nizar explained that starting in the war years, sheep and goat flocks several thousand strong would descend on this last oasis of green in a region parched by the long hot and dry summer. Everything would be eaten or trampled under a legion of cloven hooves. The long-dried pools, drained by the water pumps to irrigate the fields, would be dust bowls aching for the winter rains.

I thanked my gracious host for the coffee and followed one of the numerous goat tracks from the tent and back to the springs, the source of the marshes. Using the cracked limestone pavement as stepping stones around and over the gurgling springs, I found the mini fountains feeding a long thin pool, a temporary reservoir on the flood's journey into the wetland proper. A sluice gate, long broken, bore testimony to former days of water control. Despite abandonment, the canalized river still took much of the water eastwards under an avenue of plane trees, many broken or missing like a neglected row of teeth.

It had not been a promising start. I found a comfortable stone and sat waiting to see if dusk would bring any roosting birds. Unlike at the picnic in the summer there had been little in the way of birds through the afternoon. My notebook only recorded a handful of species; over-wintering Stonechats and Bluethroats, early migrant Reed and Sedge Warblers, Lapwing and Coot. Perhaps it was the paucity of the birds but I had not met a hunter either, although the sounds of gunshot weren't far away. But as I sat looking out over the now grey, ruffled water, the sounds of hunting and the occasional passing car on the road behind was drowned out by the cacophony of croaking from a thousand frogs.

Unexpectedly farmyard sounds cut through the amphibian mating calls. Expecting to see geese near the Bedouin tents, I soon realized the honking was above me as a flock of a hundred or so Common Cranes flew feet over my head. As I scribbled numbers in my notebook, my attention was immediately refocused as a party of a dozen pelicans, in shallow descent, a contradiction of elegance and bulk, alighted silently on the water. As the winter gloaming slowly erased the wetland, other flocks were coming into roost; a mile or so to the east, perhaps another 200 cranes, and maybe fifty more pelicans, a good way beyond the first flock. Thirty storks, probably White but perhaps with Black among them, landed nearby. Just in front of the trees the solitary splendour of a slowly flapping Spotted Eagle was just visible before it disappeared in the gloom.

And then it was a very different sound that cut through the tranquil evening. From behind the avenue a bevy of bullets spat in staccato fire, with the signature sound of machine guns slicing through the latest flock of White Storks trying to roost in the reeds. Heavy shapes tumbled from the sky but the majority of the flock lifted in unison and with extraordinary grace rose above the carnage and into the evening mist that was rolling in from the east. More bursts from the AK-47s raked the fog and reeds as the unseen hunters realized they had scared off most of their quarry. As anger welled up inside me, I knew it was time to leave. This was not a safe place to be. So, shouting loudly to alert the machine gun-wielding hunters that it was not just birds in the marshes, I ran for the car, just able to make out in the gathering gloom figures stripping the wings off dead storks and loading their bloodied corpses into the back of a military-looking jeep.

As I drove home, in some shock, I realized the Aammiq wetland was like a metaphor for Lebanon as a whole; stunningly beautiful, warmly hospitable, with overabundant life that could be extinguished with the pulling of a trigger. The landscape itself bore the scars of war and the trauma of neglect. Providing water for farmers, labourers, local villagers, and wildlife, it was taken for granted and abused. The wild open spaces that still boasted some of nature's grandest migration spectacles were also killing fields for bored soldiers.

Through Chris and Alison Walley in Beirut, the bird sightings for that day and others through the early spring were passed on to scientists assessing the importance of Lebanon's remnant refuges for wildlife. It wasn't long before word got out that Aammiq was still a great place for birds. Chris and Alison were frequent visitors, and with them and then independently, local scientists, birdwatchers and protected area programme staff came to see for themselves. These visits usually started at our place in Qab Elias and then, while Susanna prepared huge quantities of food, I would guide the groups around the wetland. With more and more people visiting, the bird records increased, supporting our initial impression that the area was still a major stopover for migrating birds and home to a rich assemblage of local residents. We often encountered lone hunters with their shotguns in frequent use but never again the militia, army, or whoever it was with the heavy guns.

Alongside the work of getting Aammiq onto the conservation map, we started the task of getting to know the locals who were equally concerned for the fate of the wetland. I would make a point of chatting to the tenant farmers that I met while on regular birdwatches and got to know the local village elders, but ironically it was through Chris's work in Beirut that we got in touch with the Skaff family – the major landowners of the Aammiq estate. Chris met Michel Skaff at a protected areas conference hosted by the United Nations Development Programme (UNDP) and was able to share with him the data we had collected showing just how rich in birdlife his land was. Michel wanted to meet this British birder, who lived in the Bekaa and took so much interest in his marsh – and there was nowhere more appropriate than the wetland itself, so a date was set to meet at the estate.

Chris and Alison came over from Beirut and we waited at *Houch Aammiq*, a collection of storerooms and stables built in the local stone around a double courtyard. Although in some need of repair, with its pitched red-tiled roof, it would not have looked out of place on a tourist brochure for Tuscany. We were not the only ones expecting to see the landlord and, as the minutes past, more and more vehicles turned up. They parked chaotically in the farmyard, their drivers clustering in animated conversation, dragging deeply on their cigarettes.

While we waited we were treated to a steady stream of Lesser Spotted Eagles, effortlessly gliding on thermals just below the late snowline of the Barouk mountain ridge to the west. Chris's telescope also picked out the occasional Short-toed Eagle, Egyptian Vulture and Steppe Buzzard, all heading north in their relentless migration drive, one of the great natural pulses of the earth. The Bekaa Valley is one of those key sites on our planet where the pulse is easiest to see. Part of a huge crack in the earth's crust, the great rift valley is a natural highway for migrating birds between their African wintering and high-latitude breeding grounds. The larger birds such as storks, eagles, and buzzards can only cover such enormous distances by relying on columns of hot air to take them high in the sky to then glide many miles with outstretched wings with only the occasional flap. These air currents do not form over water and so these majestic birds are restricted to land routes, with major bottlenecks forming where the Mediterranean, Black and Caspian Sea funnel them through the Middle East. As one of the few wetlands along the route, it is when these flocks need somewhere to roost that the Aammiq comes into its own. And here was one of the wetland's owners.

A cavalcade of jeeps turned down the avenue linking the stable complex with the main West Bekaa road. We snatched the telescope out of harm's way as the four-wheel drives swept in through the stone arch and into the first courtyard. Deep in rapid-fire French conversation, both with his travelling companion and on his mobile phone, Michel Skaff flipped into impeccable English to greet us, apologize for being late, and ask our indulgence as he had some estate business to sort before we could tour the estate and chat. Suddenly the focus switched from our small party, and the recently arrived entourage was swept into the small working office while Michel dealt with one after another of the supplicants. We drifted back to the stable gates and the identification of the raptors silently heading north, with animated Arabic bubbling behind us.

It wasn't long before Michel joined us and suggested that to get a better appreciation of the wetland we should join him on his tour of the estate, discussing our findings on the way. We crammed in the back of his battered Land Rover and shot off in the direction of the mountain ridge. To our surprise we didn't stay on the highway long but were soon bouncing around as the jeep ascended the hillside on what appeared to be a goat track with a dribble of tarmac in the middle.

It turned out that this was the decaying remains of an Israeli military road built in the 1980s by the occupying army to link their troops in the Bekaa with those stationed in the Chouf, on the other side of the mountain ridge. As we climbed higher, the tank emplacements still scarring the lower hillsides faced one another on either side of the marshes, telling the story that Michel now picked up. For much of the past decades the region had been blighted by war. At one stage the wetland was the front line between the occupying Israeli army and the Syrian forces. Village had been set against village, occupying armies had installed their positions, and tens of thousands of trees had been cut. Roads had been carved into the hills allowing the ever-hungry goats into the forests, clearing wide swathes of cover. Many inhabitants of the West Bekaa had left for Beirut, the Gulf or further afield. Like many others, the Skaff family now lived in Beirut, managing the estate from afar.

We had arrived at Ain el Ahed, one of the major mountain springs and the high point of the estate. Spreading below us, the road dropped precipitously, snaking between rock slides and grey sculptured boulders that had tumbled from the higher crags. Steeply sloping meadows punctuated with pillar box red anemones cascaded down to a wadi, its northern flank a line of limestone cliffs wearing their corsages of purple *aubretia*. Holm Oak forest covered the steepest slopes and Umbrella Pine woodlands blurred the divide between the hillside and the penny plain flat of the Bekaa. To the south we could see Lake Qaraoun, nearly filling the valley with the towns of the West Bekaa like toy villages far below us. To the east the great brooding mass of Mount Hermon dominated all, its soft whipped peaks building to the smooth snowy summit, lost in wispy cloud.

We were just below the late snow and it wasn't long before another pulse of migrating birds on huge but silent wings floated past us. Being eye to eye with a Griffon Vulture and looking down on the arching magnificence of an Imperial Eagle, its wing coverts and neck glistening, golden flecks on its ebony aerofoil, was deeply humbling. Even as we gazed, dumb in wonder, a column of spiralling White Storks was lifting from the wetland far below. Having spent the night in the relative safety of meadows, ringed by water or fringed from view by reeds, they were now ready to continue their epic journeys, gaining height as quickly as possible to take them out of the range of the hunters' guns.

In hushed tones Michel explained that through the war years management of the estate had been deeply difficult. There were periods of exile – family members scattered abroad – and periods when the area was off-limits, the wrong side of a newly drawn military boundary. In the vacuum it was not just the armies that had taken a toll. In war, opportunists move in and the wetland edges had been nibbled away year after year as field boundaries were illegally extended. Contracts were given by unscrupulous middlemen exposing the area to the grazing juggernaut of huge flocks of sheep and goats. Hunting had become a way of life, a cathartic release from the angst of war. But the family were keen to leave the chaos of the war years behind them, to establish a viable management of their land that provided a fair income and employment while preserving the jewel, tarnished as it was, of the West Bekaa. They wanted a living as well as a working landscape where the excesses of corruption no longer threatened the integrity as well as the beauty of their inheritance. Michel continued that every year the water table was dropping, soil was being lost at unprecedented rates, and fewer and fewer birds were seen. But today was a day of hope, and for our part we agreed to keep monitoring the birds and mobilizing for protection. The Skaff family were keen to involve the conservation movement in their task of bringing Aammiq back to the nature reserve it was once and could be again.

As well as exploring the country to supplement the children's historical education, we added biology to the curriculum and many Naylor family outings were planned around birdwatching at the wetland or exploring other secrets of the Aammiq estate. The trickle of visitors became a flood and we were soon hosting and guiding increasing numbers around the West Bekaa – finding the best spots to show them breeding Long-legged Buzzards, or where to catch a glimpse of Wild Boar, Golden Jackal, or fishing egrets. RSPB wardens on sabbatical, academics, local school teachers, ambassadors (always with a retinue of security guards), politicians, and many local friends and neighbours were some of the early eco-tourists we showed around. Ironically many of the most local friends we made, living in the villages of the West Bekaa, knew little of the natural delights of the wetland. Building our case for conservation, we got to know the local village *mukhtars* and other community leaders, introducing them to their very own National Geographic film set. It wasn't until I met Tony, the student son of one of the local village elders, that I understood why so little was known locally about the marshes and their surroundings.

Tony was keen to improve his English and his father, the local *muktar*, did not think it safe that I should go alone into the wetland. I was happy to have company and realized if the marsh had any future, local people needed to value it, so I was always keen to show people around. Early in the morning on the appointed Saturday in July, Tony was waiting for me at the springs, ready for the now weekly early morning bird count. He was clearly nervous and insisted that we armed ourselves with the huge sticks he had brought. Somewhat perplexed, I humoured him and we set off for the bird walk, armed with our cudgels. As the light grew stronger and the heat started to build, Tony became more relaxed and opened up in response to my question: "What are the sticks for?"

"There are many dangerous things in the wetland," he replied with a knowing frown.

"The feral dogs can be a real problem," I agreed, "but I keep stones in my pocket to scare them off, and they are rarely in the wetland."

"The sticks aren't for them, it's for the *nimir*," Tony patiently explained to his dimwitted companion. "But we won't be bothered, now. It is too hot."

I knew from Sam's Arabic primer that *nimir* meant tiger and that the nearest tigers were thousands of miles away in India. I explained this to Tony.

"Yes," he said, "but there is something like it here. Some people say it is like a tiger, others that it is a lion. I have seen pictures of a dead one that looks like its jaw can shoot forwards out of its mouth and harpoon you."

In further conversations with Tony and his friends, it became clear there was real reluctance to enter the wetland or other desolate places. Rumours of savage beasts almost certainly came from rare sightings of the Jungle Cat (only likely to do you any damage if you were a bird), or the Striped Hyena – fearsome-looking but a harmless scavenger. Hints were also dropped of darker reasons to avoid these lonely places. Local superstition pointed to the activity of Jinn or evil spirits far from human eyes, but these were also bad places for keeping your reputation intact as very earthly assignations were also kept there in the hours of darkness.

This local reluctance to enter the wilder places of the Bekaa was in stark contrast to the hunters, who knew the forests and hills, mountain and marshes well. Often with an encyclopedic knowledge of the natural history of the region, the serious hunters were scathing of the "townie" hunters (whether they came from Beirut or the local village) who shot at anything that moved, often from their balcony or car. Faisal was one such experienced hunter who had come to note the growing rarity of his quarry. Increasingly tracking in the hills simply to find and watch local wildlife rather than kill it, he became a firm friend and guide, taking the family to see roosting Barn Owls in bombed-out houses, Fire Salamander tadpoles in the mountain springs, chameleons that would crawl up the children's clothes, and exquisite orchids deep in the marsh.

Josh marked just how well the biology lessons were going when, at just over a year old, he called out "Stork!" and correctly identified the passing migrants. He precipitated a rush of visiting birders to get their binoculars and pour out onto our balcony where he had been playing.

CHAPTER 6

Mission Impossible

1996–98
The Bekaa Valley, Lebanon

It was eight o'clock on a cloudless Sunday morning in May and there was a queue of thirty-five children waiting patiently at our back door. One per step, they spiralled down our concrete stairs to the school playground below.

It was my fault. Last week, as I handed out our very last coloured crayon to Ali, I had said that from now on we could only take the first thirty children who came for Sunday school. So a week later, with two hours to go, the younger children waited, marking their places like eager shoppers on the eve of the London sales. The older boys were playing football in the schoolyard, no doubt planning to push in when the doors opened at ten.

"So now what are we going to do?" asked Susanna. "We can't leave them waiting on the steps. It is already getting warm; the ones in the sun will get heatstroke."

"What about if we take a register now, and send them away? Then at ten, if their names are written down, they can come in," I suggested, still clinging to my illusion of order.

"And you are really going to turn away the kids that come at the normal time? Look," Susanna went on, "little Hadije is there. She never comes without Maryam; she will be saving a place for her.

And those boys playing football have to be let in if their sisters, queueing on the steps, are to come in. At least it's a good problem to have," comforted Susanna as we made our way down the steps, telling the kids they could all come back at ten and we would start Sunday Club as normal.

When we signed up to work with the church in the Bekaa we never thought it would be so easy to teach Bible stories in the village. What had started as a club for our kids and their friends mushroomed quickly into a major children's ministry of the Presbyterian Church of Lebanon and Syria in our front room, and dining room, and children's bedrooms. Today it spilled out onto the large balcony in front of the apartment. Our own children struggled with the weekly invasion of their home (and toys) but the village kids, with very little to occupy them, loved it.

And so today, with children's Arabic choruses reverberating round the apartment, groups of six or seven children kneeled around huge sheets of cardboard and with pencil, crayon, and paint they were creating scenes from the biblical and Qur'anic story of Noah. The children's names identified them as coming from either the Christian or Muslim corners of the village. But without rancour Muhammad painted the ark with Tony while Leila and little Maggie were working on a pair of camels.

Life was full. As well as teaching and chaplaincy work at the school and the life of a young family, a whole field of opportunity had opened up in the village. Sunday morning was open home and Bible teaching. Through the week we had a near-constant stream of visitors, children and adult, through the house. Whereas in England polite conversation shies away from anything personal, the opposite might be said of the Lebanese village. To be polite you need to show you care about your neighbours, and if you care about them you talk about things that matter to them.

This extends to subjects which are nearly taboo in the English context – religion, for example. In the UK it seems to have been decided that religion is personal and so must be kept out of all conversation. Not only is religion personal it is also serious or, even worse, a subject people feel strongly about. As Kate Fox points out in her masterly book *Watching the English* one of our most profound rules is "The Importance of Not Being Earnest".[19] Not so for our Lebanese neighbours. Religion was clearly important to us – it must be, as we worked for the church; so they asked us about our faith – a lot.

So it didn't come as a surprise when Abu Charbel, one of the elders of the local church, asked me: "So what is this birdwatching all about? Shouldn't you be spending your time teaching the Bible, not birdwatching?"

Only slightly taken aback, as we had mostly come to terms with the fact that our neighbours knew pretty much everything we did, I replied, "I do teach the Bible. We had forty children in Sunday school this morning."

"Glad to hear it, but you are a man of religion. If you have time to watch birds, you have too much time. After your work at the school and time with the family, any free time should be spent working for the church, teaching the Bible."

The term *Rajul id deen* (man of religion) was stamped in my passport – it was on the basis of my work with the church and school that we had residency in the country. It was clearly my defining identity as far as Abu Charbel saw it and should dictate how I spent my time.

As a quick retort I quoted Jesus' injunction in Matthew's Gospel: "Look at the birds of the air."[20]

But the conversation had got me thinking. Abu Charbel had touched a raw nerve. We had come to the Middle East to work with the church. We had gone to Bible college, learned Arabic and raised financial support to live out our faith in the communities of the West Bekaa. We had sacrificed the simpler realities of English schools to work in and educate our children, a free and world-

---

[19] Kate Fox, *Watching the English*, London: Hodder & Stoughton, 2014, p. 62.
[20] Matthew 6:26, NIV, UK 2011.

class health care service, and extended family life for a tougher life with only sporadic electricity, intermittent water, and military bombardment just down the valley. Was this all so that I could birdwatch?

The answer to my questions and a radical redefinition in my understanding of what it meant to work for the church came in two instalments. Part one came when I took my Year 9 class on a field trip to the wetland. We were studying ecology in the classroom, learning how natural ecosystems provide for human needs: clean water, soils, fish and game, fuel and natural pharmaceuticals. It seemed only right to take them to the closest thing left in the valley to a natural system; and so on one of the last days of the summer term I was in a hot school bus with forty exuberant teenagers on our way to Aammiq. We were still in Zahle, less than half a mile from the school, when the Derbakeh drums came out. No Lebanese school trip is complete without the rolling beat of these drums, picked up by the open hand claps of the class egging on a dancer or two in the aisle. Sugary pastries, sweets, chocolate, and cola were soon on offer as forty snack boxes were plundered. By the time we arrived at the wetland, the class was buzzing.

With my fellow teachers I lined the students up on the grass by the bus for a stern lecture about respecting the wildness and tranquillity of the wetland. We were guests of the landowners who had kindly given permission for the trip; you could even say we were guests of the wetland itself. They were to walk carefully down to the trees lining the first pool, carrying the equipment needed for the day, clipboards, pond nets and plastic bowls, in single file on the narrow track.

The enforced calm lasted until the first of the insects were spotted. The students at the front of the line had pushed their way through a patch of long grass, disturbing a group of cone heads, large grasshopper-like creatures with long extended heads. With wide wings of gauze, they flew just a few yards after the disturbance, to settle once again in the long grass and on the children.

There were immediate cries of: "Kill it!", "It's on me!", "Aghhhhh!" echoing round the wetland. The orderly line exploded. Dancing to a very different beat, the students eventually made it to the rendezvous under the trees and after several minutes of remonstrating, comforting, and checking that there were no insects in hair or clothes, the class was quiet.

As order was restored, a shadow of silver floated over the group. All heads looked up and they sat transfixed, gazing at the suspended form of a Short-toed Eagle, its cinnamon head stock still, the paleness of its body and wings in constant motion. It was hunting for snakes. I decided not to mention that to my nervous class, but just to let the experience of the encounter work its magic. A connection was being made. This group of urbanized, processed food-fuelled young people were connecting with some of the deeper realities of the universe, with majesty and aching beauty, as a truly wild hunter briefly shared its space with them.

Taking the opportunity of the calm that had descended on the class with the appearance of the eagle, we divided the students into three groups. Mr Bsous took one group for a hike up the nearby slope of Qalaat Mudiiq to look for tortoises, lizards, and geckos. Faisal, who had joined us for the afternoon, took the second group to look for birds in the receding pools, beyond the reed bed. I gathered my dozen or so pupils to trawl the deeper pool by the trees to discover what delights lived under the water, using our improvised pond nets of old stockings and bent coat hangers.

It was a transformed class that reconvened under the shade of the ash tree a couple of hours later. They were bubbling with information about the creatures they had seen; the iridescence of the cockchafer beetles, the drunken flight of the Scarce Swallowtail butterfly, and the sheer fun of catching the tadpoles and miniature frogs soon to begin their lives on land. Using their own observations, it was like conducting an orchestra to establish the learning objectives of the lesson; the wetland provided invaluable services to the human communities of the Bekaa, it contained rare and beautiful species and it needed protection.

We didn't stop there; questions tumbled from the class all the way back to the bus. Why was the wetland so special? What had happened to the rest of the wildlife of the valley? Why were there so many types of insects? Why did God bother making so many types of beetles, and why were they so beautiful? Why did the eagle have to hunt; to kill to live?

We picked up some of the questions in biology lessons and others in chapel, but what the experience taught me was that the wetland, the wild places of Lebanon, had a power to teach – science, yes, but also much deeper subjects. I shouldn't have been surprised. The psalms are full of creation pointing to God, and the book of Job, chapters 38 to 41, has Job learning his "mystery of the universe" lessons by observing nature and some of its more extraordinary creatures. But in contemporary life these encounters are rare. The students of Zahle were more fortunate than many as they lived in a spectacular landscape, but they were still more familiar with the shopping mall than the mountain and spent more time in a virtual computer world than the hills. Even if they went into those hills they would seldom see an eagle, or have the chance to find a tortoise. Local wildlife was on the brink of extirpation and the orchestra of creation praising God and pointing to him, written about in Psalm 148, was rapidly being silenced as more and more species became extinct.

The second instalment in my redefinition of the work of the church came with a visitor, or two visitors to be precise.

Chris and Alison often arranged for the visits of scientists, conservationists, and policymakers to the wetland and that generally meant a stay at our apartment, at least for a meal. The visitors usually came from Beirut and stayed for lunch. These visitors were coming from Portugal and might stay... well, Chris wasn't sure. In any event they were welcome, particularly when we discovered that they had founded the first-ever Christian field studies centre and a conservation organization called A Rocha near a wetland on the Algarve.

Peter and Miranda Harris spent what turned out to be nearly a week with us. It started off innocently enough. I was delighted to meet a fellow birder who both knew his Mediterranean birds and had thought through many of the theological issues I was grappling with as a newbie Christian worker. Susanna was delighted that Miranda was *not* a birder and that she took an instant and real shine to our children. The kids loved visitors, particularly the rare kind who read them stories, and they enjoyed the family picnics arranged to show the visitors the wonders of our corner of paradise.

With the children playing in the stream and Susanna and Miranda comparing notes on cross-cultural living at opposite ends of the Mediterranean, Peter and I were sitting quietly on a promontory overlooking the Ras el Ain gorge, just above the village, where I had promised Peter we would see Western Rock Nuthatch. We had heard the liquid trill already so knew that the birds were around, but as yet had not had a sighting of these rock acrobats, wearing their highwayman masks.

I used the pause in activity to ask Peter what he felt about Abu Charbel's jibe, which still bothered me. After hearing me out, Peter replied, "You are breaking the mould. Abu Charbel, like many others, thinks the church should keep to traditional areas of work. Teaching the Bible, pastoral work, education, and perhaps medical relief. Of course, even if that is your starting point, the environmental crisis is now so serious that there are more refugees from ecosystem breakdown than war, and the church needs to get involved."

"But what about priorities?" I pressed. "What is the most important thing? Preaching, poverty relief, or conservation of rare species?"

"It is very rarely either/or, certainly at a community level. And that is how we should be working. A church that doesn't have an answer to today's biggest issue will not be listened to for anything else. But even that is pragmatic. At root it's about obedience. God commanded us to look after the creation for him, and it is by doing what we were created to do that we worship. We worship by being obedient."

Things were clicking into place. "And that is how creation worships. I mean plants, animals, even rocks – matter! Matter matters because it can worship by being what it was created to be – do what it was created to do.

"And that is the heresy of extinction," Peter went on. "There is an extermination of species due to human activity that has pushed the extinction rate to a thousand times the normal. We are silencing the choir that should be singing glory to God. Think about conservation projects that demonstrate God's love for his created world, protect the environment for the poorest communities, and give opportunity to explain the 'why' – why is the church saving an orchid – to those of faith and to those of no faith."

Before the conversation could get more personal, I was saved by the Western Rock Nuthatch which made an appearance on a rocky ledge on the opposite wall of the gorge.

We continued to delight in showing Peter and Miranda our new world and they continued to open up a bigger one for us – or more accurately, this one, but looked at through a biblical lens. Just before they left, Peter and Miranda had one more surprise for us.

"We think it looks like you have the makings of an A Rocha project here," said Peter, as we drank our after-dinner coffee, having cleared the plates and children from the table.

"There are the key ingredients of the recipe," Miranda continued. "A precious wildlife haven crying out for conservation, with Christians working through their theology at the spearhead of a community trying to save it."

This was not too much of a surprise, as we had been talking through the week of the possibilities of conservation, environmental education, and even eco-tourism at the marsh, learning from the A Rocha experience in Portugal. But Peter and Miranda had saved their bombshell to the end. "And we think you are the right couple to lead it."

Looking back, we had left ourselves wide open but thought they must be shell shocked from the nightly bombing we were hearing from just down the valley, as it was a particularly active time for cross-border tension. Whatever the cause we promised to think, pray, and talk to Interserve and our home church in the UK, but despite significant trepidation we also recognized a deep sense of "rightness", a fit between the task and where we found ourselves geographically, professionally, but more than anything else, theologically.

Friends, family, Interserve, and Peter and Miranda helped us work through the trepidation, and so at the start of the new academic year, I met with the school principal to explain the new opportunity, which meant I would only be working for one more year at the school. He was somewhat pacified as two new British teachers had joined the school and I promised that we would be developing an environmental education programme at the wetland, with the Zahle schools at the front of the queue. Don and Nicola Alexander and Nicholas and Catherine Morris had not just joined the school community, they had come to live in Qab Elias and proved to be an invaluable support to us, as joining the conservation efforts in the valley meant embarking on an exciting but deeply challenging road for us all.

Our second year in the valley was one of putting down roots. With a clear sense of purpose, we became more embedded in the community. We made connections with the villages around the wetland, conservation groups in Beirut, and schools and colleges in the valley. As we became more involved in the community concerns around us, so we became more at home in our adopted culture. Our days, weeks, and months followed Lebanese rather than British rhythms. We celebrated new feasts, noted new fasts, and marked the year in Middle Eastern time.

Daily routine was shaped by the debilitating heat of the afternoon. For much of the year mid-afternoon was searingly hot and so work needed to happen early. Schools were typical with an early start at eight in the morning. By two o'clock, the school bell would have sounded and a stampede of students would career down the school paths to the waiting buses poised to take them to the towns and villages of the Bekaa. The more populous destinations would be served by huge American-style buses, gaudily painted in the school colours. Being the heavyweights of the fleet, they would take pole position nearest to the school gates, revving their engines and honking their horns to speed the willing children to their waiting seats. Smaller groups would make their way to the battered minivans, their taxi drivers having slept the day away on the back bench seats while their passengers learned their lessons. In no less of a hurry, they would weave their way between groups of children boarding the bigger buses and the occasional private car, as eager as everyone else to get home and to be fed.

Particularly in summer, the heat of the afternoon is used for sleeping. It would often only be a short siesta, however, as the students would have hours of homework. Many of their parents would then go to tend their *basatiin* (usually translated "gardens" but market gardens would be more accurate) or to give a couple of hours to a second, usually family job.

The evenings were for visiting and relaxing. The TV would be on, whether in the house or on the patio, the dialogue drowned out by the noise of gossip and laughter. Supper would be light and communal – shared with visitor and family alike. Older men might be smoking while playing *tawli* (backgammon) on exquisite squares of Syrian marquetry. The women would more than likely be preparing more delicious snacks and pastries, with young children playing games by the table or dozing under a chair, the teenagers locked in Herculean efforts to memorize more chapters of literature or, if they had finished, flirting with friends under the watchful eyes of *Taite* (Grandma), wizened by her years in the sun.

This very biological pulse was not the only active rhythm. For many, a litany of prayer marked their day. Muslim neighbours would rise just before dawn to be ready for the first call to prayer.

Prayer mats spread, they would be on their knees bowing towards Mecca long before we woke. In the summer this could be very early, and so they might try to catch some sleep before rising for the start of work. The rest of the day was divided by four more calls to prayer from the mosques, broadcast from speakers all over the town and answered by obeisance wherever the faithful found themselves. Our greengrocer would shut up shop, truck drivers would pull off the road, and neighbours and friends would find their own solutions to the imperative to pray. Midday and mid-afternoon required minor adjustments in the flow of business. The sunset and night-time prayers were more private affairs conducted in the sanctity of the home.

As non-Muslims, we were only really fully aware of this other religious rhythm during the month of Ramadan when the Islamic pulse was at its most communal. Living in a mostly Muslim neighbourhood, we were visited by the *misaharati* (Ramadan drummer) at four in the morning. A human alarm clock, he would bang on his drum and, at the top of his voice, sing songs of praise to God to wake the Muslim faithful. This was well before dawn, as the wake-up call was not for the first prayer of the day, but for their *suhuur* meal, the last chance to eat or drink prior to the daylight hours of fasting.

Outside all but the most completely Christian communities, working days were shortened during Ramadan and it was more difficult to get business done as so many colleagues were sleepy. From around half an hour before sunset, you tried to make sure you were home safely and most definitely not on the road. The traffic would be more manic than usual, with hungry and tired drivers battling the jams to get home by *iftar*, the breaking of the fast and family celebration meal.

It was always a real delight and privilege to be invited to a family *iftar*. Everyone was in high spirits. The adults' twelve-hour fast was coming to an end, throughout which they had not even had a glass of water. Children would be excitedly running between relatives, looking forward to the feast their mothers and aunts had worked on for most of the afternoon. With the call from the mosque, a howl of delight would rise from the youngest, and sweet sugary fruit drinks would be passed round, to be followed by crisp salads, steaming bread with eggplant dips, and fat juicy olives suffused with lemon and garlic. These were just the warm-up act. The main event of rice piled into mountains bejewelled with pomegranate seeds, almonds and pistachios and surmounted with succulent chicken or lamb, would follow. The evening would pass in a haze of food, eventually drawing to a close with fruit, coffee, and *lakoum* (known as Turkish Delight in the West). As we finally fell into bed, the thought that our gracious hosts would be getting up at four the next morning was humbling. We would drop off to sleep profoundly grateful that we could ignore the early morning drumbeats.

In Lebanon, our weekly rhythm was much more like a British working week than in many parts of the Middle East. Typically throughout the region, Friday was the day when offices, schools, and businesses closed. However, in Lebanon, although government offices would have reduced working hours on a Friday, the weekend observed by most was Saturday and Sunday. But whereas the weekly beat was a Western one, the yearly cycle was an eclectic compilation of religious feasts that left no one out. They included:

- Two New Year's days (1 January, and the Islamic New Year)

- Two Christmas days (Western, and Armenian on 6 January)

- The Prophet Mohammed's birthday

- Annunciation Day

- Good Friday

- Two Easters (Western and Eastern)

- *Eid el Fitr* at the end of Ramadan

- The Assumption of the Virgin Mary

- *Eid el Adha* (the feast of the sacrifice, honouring Abraham)
- *Ashoura* (honouring the martyrdom of Hussein, the Prophet's grandson, particularly significant to the Shia)
- St Maroun's day (the founder of the Maronite Church)[21]

Simply following the lunar cycle, the Islamic calendar is ten to eleven days shorter than its Western equivalent and so the Islamic feasts shift through the Western calendar each year. Whereas Christmas is always in the northern winter and Easter in the spring, Ramadan, *Eid el Fitr* and the other Islamic feasts progress through the seasons, occasionally bringing the sects together in celebration of very different traditions.

---

[21] Following political events from 2000, a number of new holidays have been added, including Liberation of the South day and The commemoration of PM Rafik Hariri's assassination.

CHAPTER 7

"*Salaam Alaykum* and Thanks Be to God"

1998–2000
The Bekaa Valley, Lebanon

We had been living in what the children called "the lovely ugly house" for nearly a year. With rapid developments in the growing A Rocha project, we needed more space; space for visitors (now a constant stream), space for meetings, an office, and space for the growing family. Our first international team members had joined us in the form of West Coast Canadians Karin and Alain Boisclaire-Joly. With humbling commitment they were literally on their honeymoon as they moved into our old apartment above the school and we moved to the edge of the village, to the Hakim House facing the main West Bekaa road and backing on to the landscape of overgrazed hillsides that surround Qab Elias.

Bayt Hakim had been built by the father of two elderly sisters who left for their homes in the States after agreeing to rent the family summer home to the "foreign family in the Bekaa". It had been a long drawn-out negotiation over the course of the summer. We were taking part in a final chapter, watching the closing scene in a story of emigration and loss.

The house was the last link with the "old country" for a Maronite family whose grandchildren only spoke English with an American twang and knew the family home through photographs carried by the elderly matriarchs who returned each summer. But this would be their last visit. They wanted to sell the house to us because we were Christians and they wanted to preserve their faith heritage on the land. Eventually, after getting to know us through their summer swansong, they agreed that we could rent the house, with a warning that they would sell if they could, but not yet, as the Christians weren't buying. It was still too unsettled politically to buy.

The house was as eccentric as its first owner. Monsieur Hakim had been the headmaster of the local high school, who practised a pupil-centred philosophy well beyond the classroom. When a former student graduated as an architect and needed a first project to launch his career, Mr Hakim awarded him the contract to design his family home. The result was an oversized grey cube dropped on the hillside, set back from the road by an equally square terraced garden. The central double door with four symmetrical windows, marking the two storeys, only confirmed the impression that the blueprint had been a child's sketch. The engineering appeared naive too, as the house was slowly sinking into the hillside. There were wide cracks on the south-facing side and the external walls did not meet the floor for the entire length of the dining room.

Inside, the rooms were cavernous and cluttered as three generations had added eclectically to the contents. The furniture that had been new with the house groaned and occasionally shattered in explosions of dust in sympathy with the building. An enormous gothic wood-framed mirror borrowed light for the hall, but dark-stained bookcases, desks, and wardrobes sucked up any illumination that got through the heavy curtains in the lounge and dining room. In the family room, a forbidding scarlet sofa with matching 1950s purple armchairs lounged drunkenly, leering with the pitch of the floor.

Like most houses in the Bekaa, it had been built for the summer, when heat was the enemy and must be excluded from the home. The local wildlife certainly thought of the house as a cool haven, a square cave with convenient access points for ease of entry. If we had guests it was usually the tarantulas that caused the greatest commotion. Squeezing through the gap between the wall and the floor, they would scuttle over feet in their dash for the dark recesses under the monolithic furniture in their quest for relief from the relentless summer sun.

The family would barely twitch in response to the tickle of spider feet on their own, but it was a different story with the centipedes. A full inch wide and eight inches long, they packed a powerful punch or, to be precise, a painful bite: the children left them well alone. The same could not be said for most of the wildlife, however. Whether they came in under their own steam or were rescue projects brought to us by neighbours, the children delighted in some unusual pets: big hairy spiders, geckos, lizards, snakes, tortoises, a bat, a mole rat (think hairy sausage with awesome teeth), and everyone's favourite: chameleons.

All three children responded as only children can who have not been taught to fear creepy-crawlies by the adults around them – with passionate interest and respect. They also enjoyed them in their own unique ways. Sam's interest was primarily academic: "What is it called? What is it related to, and how does it fit into the ecosystem?" Chloe, in contrast, was very "hands-on". A mother hen, she would look after her miscellaneous brood, meeting their real and imagined needs. Joshua, an inquisitive toddler, wanted to enter the world of the animals. This frequently meant that he would escape the confines of the garden and join the herds of sheep and goats on the hillside around the house. If he was missing, the first place to look for his blond curls was with the shepherds, who loved his company – another charge in their flock.

I had just retrieved Josh, once more smelling of goat, from the latest passing herd, and had repaired the fence that was supposed to keep him in, when I joined Susanna watching history on the veranda at the front of the house. Our home-school history project had taught us that people movements had long been a feature of the region. The very fact we could rent the house we were living in was a result of one of the most recent demographic shifts – the haemorrhage of Christians from the Middle East. What we were watching from our terrace was more like a river in spate, as a caravan of humanity poured south along the main Bekaa highway. Bumper to bumper cars, trucks, minibuses, and lorries sped south, horns blaring and flags waving, jubilant.

After eighteen years, Israel had hurriedly and unilaterally withdrawn from the approximately 10 per cent of Lebanese territory it had been occupying since the 1980s. Like a wind rushing to fill a vacuum, Shiite Muslim communities, long displaced, poured back home. The cavalcade went on for hours as exultant families, with all their possessions packed into whatever vehicle that would carry them, returned to reclaim their birthright.

This was an entire community on the move, carrying the same flags and banners that marked their adopted territory in the years they were settled to the north. We would see the same identity markers as we drove through the mosaic of sects that made up the Bekaa. It was always easy to know whose territory you were driving through, as each group had its own street icons establishing its character, so that no one could be in any doubt of its ownership.

When we travelled north, on the same road that was currently taking the human caravan southward and home, we would first drive through the largely Sunni Muslim towns of Makse and Chtaura. In striking distance of the Syrian border crossing, commerce dominated here, with Western-style supermarkets providing convenience food to the Syrian elite who flocked across to fill their shopping trolleys. Religion played second fiddle as enormous billboards promised fulfilment in the form of washing powders, Japanese electronics, and Scotch whisky. The adverts were as likely to be in English as Arabic as this was the Bekaa *à l'américaine*.

The street language changed a few miles up the road, coming into Saadnayel, and was even more strident further to the north in Baalbek. Territory was claimed here by the green and yellow of Hezbollah, the dominant political force of the Shiite community in the valley. The highway was punctuated every 100 yards or so by sombre, black-edged posters strapped to lampposts, featuring earnest young faces, still growing into their beards, staring down at the passing traffic, immortalized on paper but forever missing from their families. Icons of a very different martyr marked the Christian avenues of Ksara and Zahle. The sacrificial hands of Christ welcomed you to these streets, along with assorted saints and the cross, the most potent symbol of sacrifice of all. The markers were clear and cumulative, designed to proclaim belief and identity, separating communities even if only a few hundred yards apart.

But what about the communities themselves? What did they believe? I learned how Muslims felt about their faith from our neighbours and friends. Hassan, a close new neighbour, was our first guide. For his day job he taught Arabic at the local school, but he was also a keen businessman and passionate hiker. When he found out that I knew the paths above Aammiq and had permission from the landowners to walk the trails, he booked his next free Saturday to join me on our monthly biodiversity survey of the mountain. Bright and early, we started at the mouth of the wadi, from where the footpath snaked its way to the top of the Barouk ridge, some 1,000 metres and several hours upwards.

Pausing to note birds and butterflies, we followed the same route I took each month, cataloguing the seasonal changes. As well as Masked Shrikes, Hoopoes, and Adonis butterflies, the other great joys of these walks were the panoramic views and the wide-ranging conversations with travelling companions. There is something about stepping out into nature's grandeur that leads to honesty and openness in discussion. Certainly I learned more from my conversations with Hassan on the mountain than I did in the social constraints of his formal lounge.

Hassan was in contemplative mood as we ate the apricots he had brought from his garden in the shade of the great oak, known locally as *Shajarit is Sitt* (the tree of the old woman). We were looking north along the hanging valley, parallel to the floor of the Bekaa far below. The tectonic lines of the landscape drew our eyes up to the glistening frozen heights of Mount Sannine, looming above Zahle to the north.

"Islam is the natural religion of the world. You just need to recognize God and submit to him. Islam means submission, and Muslim, the one who submits," Hassan stated.

"Yes, I know, Hassan," I replied. "We have a lot in common. But to become a Muslim I would have to say the Shahadah: *'Ashhadu an la ilaha illa-llah, Muhammada rasulu-llah'*, wouldn't I? [I bear witness that there is no god except God and that Mohammed is the messenger of God.] I have no problem with the first bit, but the problem I have with the second part is minor in comparison to the problem you have with Jesus."

"We hold the prophet Isa, or Jesus as you call him, in the highest regard. Did you know we believe that he was born of a virgin?" countered Hassan.

We had finished our apricots, and by unspoken but mutual consent decided that the conversation was getting tense and would go more smoothly if we continued our hike. Initially an easy stroll through a gently sloping meadow, we were soon catching our breath, the path gaining height rapidly with our approach to the spring of Ain Salouk. Throughout our exertions, Hassan continued his evangelistic lesson in Islam.

"So you know the first act of Islamic worship – our creed, the Shahadah. Do you know all five?" he asked.

"Prayer (five times a day), fasting, giving alms to the poor, and pilgrimage to Mecca.[22] You have been on the Hajj, haven't you? What's it like?" I asked, keen to reduce the intensity of the conversation.

---

[22] Sometimes referred to as the Five Pillars of Islam.

Hassan's face took on a beatific smile as he said quietly: "Wonderful. It was the highlight of my life. Just imagine, you take off every distraction. Simply wearing two white cloths, you join a never-ending stream of pilgrims, equal in worship, no matter their rank or wealth back home. You might be next to a king or a pauper, you wouldn't know. We were all the same as we circled the *kaba'a*, the sacred house. We were specks in the universe, dots in time, insignificant in the face of God's glory."

"That's the real difference between Islam and Christianity, right there," I said. "I love the display of equality, the unity is awe-inspiring in the rites of the Hajj, but for me Jesus brings significance. By taking on flesh and blood, God invested himself in the stuff of us, and that changed everything."

We had reached the top of the ridge. To the west the ground fell away like a crumpled sheet through the Chouf hills and on to the Mediterranean, sparkling in the afternoon sun. Facing us like ancient sentinels, a grove of cedar trees partly obscured the view. It was claimed that the oldest of the trees would have been saplings when Christ walked the streets of Tyre and Sidon, just a few miles along the coast below us. These monumental trees, so beloved by the Lebanese, reminded us how both the Bible and Qur'an came out of the ecosystems of the Middle East. Both holy books refer to the trees as archetypes of strength and vigour.[23] It seemed an appropriate end to the hike as we stopped talking and just feasted on the beauty of the forest trees silently lifting their powerful boughs in their own supplication and worship to God.

And then we had to walk back to the car!

It was Bilal, another friend, and my barber, who gave me insight into the vexed question of the Sunni–Shia divide at the heart of Islam.

It was a slow afternoon, so Bilal was paying even more attention than normal to his trade. A Lebanese haircut is no speedy short

---

[23] For example, in the Qur'an sura LIII (*An-Najm* – The Star) verses 7–18. And in the Bible, Psalm 92.

back and sides affair. With the skill of a master craftsman and the patience and care of a surgeon, Bilal always took his time. And with time to fill, we chatted. We had been talking about why the towns and villages in the valley were either from one sect only or mixed Sunni–Christian or Shia–Christian but rarely if ever Sunni–Shia.

"What is the fundamental difference between the Sunnis and Shias?" I asked.

Bilal had spent many years in Canada, and so was used to my rather direct questions and enjoyed chatting with me about more esoteric subjects, having a Master's degree in philosophy.

"At root it is about authority and leadership. Probably around 90 per cent of all Muslims are Sunni. But soon after the Prophet's death, the seeds of division were sown with a dispute over succession and leadership. Sunnis believe that the prophet Mohammed chose Abu Bakr as his successor but we Shia believe that Ali, the Prophet's cousin and son-in-law was the rightful and chosen leader of the new community. It's a bit involved, but the first three leaders were unrelated to the Prophet, Ali only becoming the fourth caliph. He was then murdered while praying in a mosque in Kufa, Iraq. After this heinous treachery, the two communities have trod quite different paths. Sunnis have always been in the majority; the powerful, with their religious leadership, embedded in the great Muslim empires. We Shia have always looked to our imams, but they have been in the shadow of the state and we are mostly marginalized and in the minority. That is, until the Shia Islamic revolution in Iran in 1979."

And then my theological barber closed his history lesson with a remark that brought this seemingly obscure seventh-century feud, whose shadow stretched to the present day, up close and personal.

"It's not that different to your own divide between Catholics and Protestants. Sure, you have theological differences, but the reason that there is still fighting in your country, in Northern Ireland, is history; identities built up in opposition to the 'other' – power and territory, battles and persecution, alliances and treachery."

I left Bilal with a neat haircut and a lot to think about.

With all this religion squeezed into such a small country it is little surprise that common speech is peppered with blessings. Condiments of grace, they are liberally sprinkled through everyday conversations; social interactions are bathed in their appeals to the Almighty. Here are some of the most frequently heard with their literal translations and common uses:

- *Il hamdulillah*: Praise God. Used constantly and frequently in response to someone asking, "How are you?"

- *Noshkur allah*: Thanks be to God. As above.

- *Ilhamdulilah wa shukrallah*: Praise and thanks be to God. (You guessed it!)

- *Subhanallah*: Glory to God. Often used after surprise or amazement.

- *Mashallah*: What God wills. Often used for positive comment and particularly towards children.

- *Allahu akbar*: God is great. Used on many occasions, particularly to show excitement.

- *Bismallah*: In the name of God. Often used at the start of something.

- *Inshallah*: If God wills. Usually means I hope so.

- *Saluam alaykum*: Peace be upon you. Hello.

- *Wa alaykum asalam*: And on you be peace. (The reply.)

- *Allahyatiik el afeh*: God give you health. After someone has worked for you or given you something, so this one can be used when you want to get out of a taxi.

CHAPTER 8

How I Got a Gun

1999
Aammiq, the Bekaa, Lebanon

It was our fourth year in the valley and not only had we got used to the village but it had got used to us. Everybody knew who we were, if not by name, then certainly by our most commonly used title – *ajaanib*, the foreigners. We were no longer a source of endless curiosity and gossip, but simply one of the village families. Admittedly, we were a rather tiny one; the Shoukers came in their scores, the Mais family numbered hundreds, and we were five. But we were a village family.

If our family identity had been accepted, so too had Susanna and the children because they did pretty normal things such as going to school, working hard in the house, visiting neighbours, and generally keeping up with communal expectations. In fact, Susanna was working hard at home and in the village. She added to the usual heavy load of the Middle Eastern mum by working as an unpaid consultant at the children's school, helping to bring in more effective early years' teaching. She was also working in the project, keeping the accounts and giving endless advice and help to our latest volunteers and team members. Our neighbours would have been horrified if they knew how much Susanna was working, but at least they were reassured that she was doing "normal things".

The same could not be said of me. My endless days down the marsh, coming back covered in mud or dust, depending on the season, were a puzzle. Because I had been a science teacher at the local high school – and the administration told everyone that I had a degree from Cambridge University, so I was "Doctor Chris" (the first true, the second not) – the village had greater expectations from me than I was delivering. It was bad enough that I spent my time in the swamps working with shepherds, but what added serious insult was that my Arabic was starting to sound like the Bedouin I spent so much time with.

Despite the obvious disappointment I was to many, we were woven into the fabric of the village, a few white threads in a multicoloured cloth. Along with acceptance came responsibilities well described by the hugely important word in village life, *waajibat* – obligations. Many of these obligations were delightful; some were tedious; a few, deeply sad. Funerals would definitely be in the latter category. Actually, the majority we attended were not that sad for me personally, as frequently we hardly knew the deceased. That didn't matter; if we had a connection, I would have to go. The connection in question could be quite tenuous – father of my barber, cousin of our greengrocer, and mother of an ex-colleague at the Zahle school being examples that come to mind. Obligation this strong meant two things – the numbers attending funerals were huge, and I went to a lot of them.

Particularly if summer temperatures reached 40 degrees C, funerals would be thick and fast as the elderly of the village succumbed to the way of all flesh, no longer able to take the punishing heat.

My friend George's mother died in one such heatwave. She was ninety-two and had four generations of her family around her at the end, so no one was distraught at her passing. As was customary, it was just a few hours after her death and the family home had been rearranged to receive the streams of visitors who came to offer their formal condolences, with the burial the next day. With few refrigerated mortuary services, Middle Eastern funerals follow rapidly after death.

I arrived at the large family house at the other end of the village at the same time as a contingent of former colleagues from school. It was good to see them, and we were soon in animated conversation about mutual friends and the well-known characters of the classroom. As we passed under the grape arbours, gravid with clusters of purple fruit, we had quietened to hushed voices by the time we reached the door. Guided by a liveried servant, hired specially for the day, we joined the queue snaking through the entrée – a small entrance hall – shuffling forward a few paces at a time until eventually we solemnly kissed George first on his right, then left and then right cheek again, offering him our heartfelt condolences for his loss. I had hardly noticed, but the women in the group had been siphoned off, sent to an adjacent room where they muttered the same blessings to George's wife and female relatives. After greeting George, I repeated the social steps of this intricate dance of mourning with five other senior male relatives, and was then escorted by another footman to an elaborate straight-backed wooden chair, one of perhaps fifty set in a square in the imposing lounge.

Despite the heavy curtains, the summer sun brightened the room where it was allowed entrance through the net curtain covering the French doors that I knew, from previous visits, led to a courtyard garden. A delightfully flowered bower, it used to be a favourite place of George's departed mother, where she would doze her last days away. Once seated, we were quietly exchanging gossip again as we caught up on lives lived apart for several months.

George seemed tired but content. There were no tears, although there was a wistful air on the hot dry breeze coming into the last scene of a life well lived. My eyes wandered round the faces of the village, men giving up half an hour of their time for the memory of a matriarch. Christian, Muslim, and Druze: everyone was here, reverent and respectful. My reverie was distracted as a stooped and whiskered servant poured the luxuriantly bitter liquor reserved for funerals from a bronze pot engraved with elegant arabesques. Not much more than enough to wet the bottom of the tiny shot-sized coffee cup, you could feel the caffeine even as you smelled it. One sip was enough to bring the message home – *murr*: bitter, death.

Suddenly, one great side of the square got up as one and moved off out of the lounge to the main doorway. As they left the house, I could just catch the rising tempo of their voices as they re-entered the sun, the day. The village representatives were leaving behind the reminder of their own mortality. A few minutes later, I left with my companions, freeing another side of the rectangular room for the visitors still arriving in droves.

Nadine's funeral could not have been more different.

Nadine was a beautiful sixteen-year-old. We knew her family through the children's school. They lived near the Orthodox church in a three-storey family apartment block on the edge of the *basatin*, the orchards and market gardens that stretched from the village to the river. Nadine was a tomboy, she loved climbing trees, messing about in the gardens, and hunting. Her companions were a covey of cousins, all boys who lived for football and hunting.

The heatwave that had been too much for George's mother was waning and the first week of September brought cooler mornings and the first autumn migrants; Hoopoes and Honey Buzzards. Nadine had felt cooped up by the heat of August and now was her chance to really get out – not just into the gardens but into the hills. It was easy to convince Eli and Joseph to clean the guns, buy the shot, and pack the car ready for an early morning start. They drove up the valley to a spot at the end of a rutted mountain road where Joseph was happy to leave his BMW, although he was less happy with the dust that undid the hours he had just spent polishing the blue paintwork. Nadine was frustrated by how carefully Joseph drove along the track but she knew better than to complain. Joseph loved his car more than some members of the family. It was only that he loved hunting even more that meant he would take it off-road at all.

They parked, slung their shotguns over their shoulders and set off towards the wadi. Eli was in front, setting the pace with his long strides. Nadine, eager to keep up, was just behind. Suddenly Eli gesticulated for the trio to stop as he scrambled to load the gun and then swing the primed weapon up to the shadow that floated above them. He was too late; the buzzard was gone and Eli swore. Determined to be ready the next time a bird flew over, he did not break open his shotgun and kept his finger on the trigger. What he was not ready for was the slippery mud, the remnant of a tiny spring that seeped water through the summer leaving just a mat of algae this late in the season. Nadine died instantly as Eli, scrabbling to stay upright, discharged both barrels into his beloved cousin.

The funeral was as raw as the wounds that killed Nadine. As I walked through the village souk to the grieving family home, shop after shop was being shut up, the iron grilles pulled down over the store fronts as a gathering crowd moved towards the wailing that had been wafting along the high street all afternoon. There were no formalities here. A crowd surged around the courtyard in front of the house. Near the front door, rows of plastic chairs faced the open space. Here sprawled Nadine's closest female relatives, groaning and swaying, in constant danger of toppling off their chairs, gripped by a grief that prevented their limbs from working. Nadine's mother and closest aunts were propped up by younger relatives, themselves awash with tears. The source of the wailing came from a group of women in greater control of their voices, wailing in unison and beating their breasts as they swayed rhythmically side to side. The crowd gave a deeper resonant note to the requiem as a low moaning emerged etherlike from the collective sorrow.

Suddenly the tempo changed as a group of shrieking men broke into the meandering throng. They carried the coffin high above their shoulders. Mock-charging the crowd, they twisted the open casket back and forth, as if they were trying to spill its contents – daring the crowd to stop them displaying their grief by physical force. The low moaning was engulfed by shouts and screams from the jockeying rabble, hands shot out to shove the wooden box, and women at the edge of the group dropped to the floor – felled by despair. As the violence of the cortège made its way towards the gate, and in the direction of the church, it passed close enough for me to see Nadine once more. She was dressed in full bridal gown, a veil of antique white lace preserving her beauty as it obscured the ugliness of the wounds. Her face was painted as never in life, heavy make-up giving her the appearance of a life-sized doll. I stood transfixed as the procession snaked drunkenly down the road, slowly taking the entire crowd in its train.

Harrowed, I left the church an hour later. I walked home silently with Najjy, a friend and close neighbour. Just before separating and going to our own homes, I said to Najjy: "I didn't see Eli at the funeral. Was he there? How is he doing?"

"You won't see Eli for a while," Najjy replied. "He is in prison – charged with killing Nadine."

"But it was an accident. What will happen to him?" I asked, shocked.

"Difficult to say. Usually in these cases, the family of the victim wants to see some form of punishment, but Eli and Nadine were cousins, so I am not sure. I expect he will be kept for a few weeks and then the authorities will work something out with the family."

"You say usually in these cases? Does this sort of thing happen very often?" I enquired tentatively, unsure quite how much more bad news I could take.

"Unfortunately yes. There are several deaths a year in hunting accidents, but it is very unusual that it involves a girl. Usually one young friend kills another – ending one life and wrecking another."

We parted, each lost in thought.

And so we come again to the theme of hunting. The first thing to say is that this is a highly complex issue that we all come to with heavy cultural baggage. Leaving aside the Middle Eastern context for a moment, in my own country, Britain, whether you come from the town or the countryside and your social class all have enormous bearing on whether the word resonates with terms such as adventure, skill, and the great outdoors or blood, suffering, and privilege.

From a conservation perspective, there are equally varied outcomes as a result of hunting. In many parts of the world, huge areas of prime wildlife habitat have been saved for biodiversity benefit to provide a sustainable source of target species. Across North America, Ducks Unlimited, for example, has conserved more than 13 million acres of wetland since 1937.[24] Unfortunately in many countries, illegal or legal but uncontrolled hunting has pushed species after species towards extinction or local extirpation. Headline stories of rhino poaching make chilling reading, with almost two killed every day in South Africa alone. Populations have been in free fall, with black rhino numbers dropping by 96 per cent between 1970 and 1993 across Africa.[25] Huge effort has gone into reversing these trends and there has been extraordinary success, with current populations double that of the lowest years, but persistent poaching is reaching new heights and threatens these magnificent creatures with extinction once again. Of course, it is not just iconic fauna that is taking a hammering. All over the world the bush meat trade is clearing forests and wetlands, thickets and farmland of its wildlife. In Lebanon and other parts of the Mediterranean it is the birdlife that is under the fiercest threat.

In Lebanon, as elsewhere, people hunt for many different reasons. Like Nadine, Fadi hunted because he loved to get out into the hills and woods, fields and forests of the Bekaa. We met early one misty October morning when I was working with a couple of labourers, digging a pond at the edge of the Aammiq estate close to its boundary with the cedar mountain reserve.

We had parked the estate Land Rover at the chain that barred further access up the old military road into the reserve itself. Carrying our tools, we hiked from the car to the tiny stream that

[24] www.ducks.org/conservation (accessed 4.11.14).
[25] www.savetherhino.org/rhino_info/poaching_statistics (accessed 4.11.14).

trickled over the rocky terrain, largely buried along its length in a thick tangle of gorse. At this time of year water was at a real premium for migrating birds and local wildlife. The wetland, hundreds of feet below, was largely dry, the few mountain streams and spring-fed pools the only water in a parched landscape. Our bird studies had shown just how important these isolated pools were, and so we had spent the first hour of the morning clearing a patch of undergrowth and widening the stream's passage to create a shallow open pool in an area of good visibility for birds and mammals alike to drink from.

Abu Farah, Kamil and I were taking a break, enjoying the heat from the sweet tea that Kamil provided from his thermos. As Abu Farah ladled his fourth teaspoon of sugar into the steaming amber infusion, out of the mist walked Fadi. After a crescendo of greetings and kisses, Fadi drew up a rock and joined us for tea and figs. Even as we sat, the mist was clearing, rolling downhill until we were bathed in glorious autumn sunshine. The sky was a freshly washed forget-me-not blue clear across to the early snow dusting Mount Hermon's skullcap. It was as if we were in a longboat at sea. The mist had cleared from the ridge we were on and from the Anti-Lebanon hills six or seven miles to the east, but the Bekaa in between was cotton candy full, lapping a few metres below our feet.

As we enjoyed the warmth of the sun on our backs, I asked about Fadi's gun and belt.

"Where have you been hunting and what have you shot?"

Fadi knew that hunting on the Aammiq estate was forbidden, as was hunting in the cedar reserve. "Here and there," he replied. "Look what I've got!"

He proceeded to untie the string from his belt and showed us two Barn Swallows, a Tawny Pipit, a Common Redstart, and a Song Thrush.

"You know hunting is forbidden on the estate and in the reserve," I said, pointing up the hill.

"Yes, I know, but I only took a few. I could have shot three times as many. As the mist cleared, higher up the ground was hopping with birds."

I was intrigued. "So why did you only shoot these five?" I asked.

"That is all I am going to eat," Fadi replied. Then realizing he had an audience for his story, he continued, "I could have killed a Wild Boar too. I tracked the herd for an hour. I saw where they had been feeding at first light by the fresh signs on the ground. I know how they behave and where their favourite places are. They are very shy – because of the hunters – so they are very difficult to follow, but I watched them for twenty minutes foraging under the big oaks up beyond the spring. They are so beautiful, so wild."

My encounter with the Syrian general a few days later at the marsh could not have been more different. This time I was on my own and sitting in the golden light of late afternoon on the eastern side of *Qala'et el Mudiq*, the hill that was a natural vantage point for observing the most westerly area of the wetland. Once a week one of us in the team could be found sitting in the same spot an hour before sunset to just after dark, recording the birds and occasionally mammals that frequented this part of the wetland.

Although a couple of hundred yards from the reeds, I had almost stopped breathing, involuntarily making myself as still and quiet as I could, scanning the reed curtain for another glimpse of the savage grace of the Jungle Cat[26] that a few moments before had launched an ambush attack on a Lapwing that had been feeding on the last patch of drying mud. In an explosion of feathers, the delicately striped tan face was gone, as was the bird. I was alert to any movement, scanning the reeds for the merest tremble that might give away the predator's presence. What I was not expecting was the khaki green army truck that lumbered onto the short avenue of trees midway between me and the reeds, engine roaring, spewing clouds of black oily smoke from its asthmatic exhausts.

There would be no more wildlife sightings for the records

---

[26] *Felis chaus.*

this afternoon. The truck was immediately followed by an army jeep that screeched to a halt in a squeal of brakes. The tortured mechanical sounds were quickly replaced by human voices as orders were barked and an imposing figure rose from the smaller open-topped vehicle, using the height the jeep gave him as a lookout over the reed bed. A minion handed the senior officer a shotgun. I knew there were several ring-tailed harriers (either female Pallid or Montagu's – I had not had a good enough view as yet to tell which) over the eastern end of the reed bed. They would be coming into roost within range of the shotgun at any moment. I ran down the hill and into the impromptu army manoeuvre.

"Hello!" I called out in English. I often used English in these tense situations. Within the A Rocha team, we had a strict policy never to confront hunters if alone. Even with a fellow team member, we advised extreme caution. By experience I had found that the use of my poshest English accent was so out of place and farcical that it sometimes relieved what would otherwise be an aggressive encounter. Not today.

"What do you want?" the officer barked back in Arabic.

So switching to Arabic, I replied, "Well, I was going to ask you the same, sir."

For the first time he took his eyes off the marsh and the distant but approaching harrier, looking instead straight at me. "I am here to hunt – now go away. I want one of those," he said, pointing over the reeds to the quartering bird.

"I am afraid that is not allowed. You see, this is a protected area, a nature reserve."

"I know. That is why the hunting is good. You don't see these rare species everywhere. I don't have one of them. I want to add it to my magnificent collection."

At this point I noticed that while I was cleverly distracting him from taking aim, he was more cleverly distracting me from noticing that a junior officer, second shotgun in hand, was eagerly following the passage of the harrier as it zigzagged inexorably nearer.

It was like playing a game of poker. He held the stronger hand – being part of an occupying army with guns, soldiers and rank, but he didn't know what, if any, hand I held. That was my only hope of saving the exquisite thing of beauty that floated towards us as if on a light breeze. With my best poker face I decided to play both of the cards I held at once.

"I am an English scientist working on behalf of the Skaff estate. This is a very important wetland – a vital link on the world's most important migration highways for birds. It is protected by the landowners with the full backing of the international community."

The officer looked slightly less sure of himself; the soldier with the gun dropped his aim and moved closer to the conversation.

"Are you with the British Embassy?" enquired the junior officer.

"They know about the project," I replied, evasively.

The senior officer jumped down from the jeep and was soon deep in conversation with his junior colleague, just far enough away so that I could not hear.

The harrier had landed, safe, settling at the communal roost just fifty yards from the minor diplomatic incident unfolding under the plane trees.

"We have had a call from headquarters. We will go. Give our regards to the ambassador," clipped the subordinate officer, and suddenly in a swirl of activity the small band of troops were back in their vehicles and reversing out of the marsh.

As we worked more and more closely with the estate, they invested heavily in hiring local guards for the reserve. The restored habitats were full of birds and so provided the best hunting around. To combat the devastating effects of the indiscriminate hunting on the birdlife, we had a three-pronged approach. Firstly, we made access to the majority of the wetland more difficult. We ploughed up dirt tracks, dug ditches, and put chains across farm access roads to be unlocked only when farm vehicles needed to pass. This put off many, as they were not prepared to walk far, preferring to drive into the wetland in the summer and autumn before the first rains made the ground impassable. Secondly, we ran a programme particularly aimed at the youth, but also training farmers, the police and local women's groups in the importance of the wetland and the fragile state of the nation's birdlife. The last line of defence was the guards, employed to patrol the wetland and estate, to be a visible presence to deter hunters but also to challenge them if they were discovered.

Over the years, our approach, together with the commitment of the estate, had varying levels of success. In the calm years when Lebanon was at its most stable, hunting was rare and not only did migrants benefit but species that had not over-summered or bred for years were recorded extending their stay at the wetland. A few White Storks, for example, would cut their migration short and remain with us for the summer months. The first-ever breeding records of Mallard and Garganey ducks and Marsh Harriers were an enormous boost to the team and volunteers and a great indicator that the hunting and disturbance could be controlled. However, when the country was in political and military turmoil, the situation would revert to the bad old days. Frustration and fear would build and male angst would seem to be taken out cathartically on the birds. During heavy migration passage when flocks would be flying low over the valley, the gunfire would sound like popcorn bursting in a hot skillet, it was so frequent.

Most of the hunters we encountered did not have the fieldcraft of Fadi, nor the arrogance of the military trophy hunter. The majority were recreational hunters who would shoot whatever flew past – taking home what they could eat and leaving the inedible for the jackals. They would try to avoid trouble and if they met a guard or a team member out on a survey, they would apologize and go off to hunt elsewhere. A few were belligerent and confrontational, a few shot at us, and one shot one of our conservation officers (fortunately causing only a very light wound). But it was the encounter with Amer and Malik that I remember most clearly, as that is how I got my gun.

I had been at the wetland all day, working with Abu Farah and Kamil. We were setting boundary markers at the edge of the wetland, demarking where tenant farmers could plough and where they could not, on the transitional flooded pasture that was so rich a habitat for wildlife. It was coveted by tenants who could pay a rent for 100 *dunum* and plough up 110, and so year by year eat away at the marsh. The markers in question were enormous iron poles set deep in the ground. The idea was to make moving them nigh on impossible. They were ugly and modern but they went with the spirit of Proverbs 22:28, "Don't cheat your neighbor by moving the ancient boundary markers set up by previous generations."[27]

Throughout the day there had been spectacular flocks of birds of prey on their epic journeys south and as conditions were calm and hunting minimal, I had a hunch that as we went into the late afternoon we would have significant numbers dropping in to roost at the marsh. I was determined Susanna would see this wildlife spectacle. She had been working on the project accounts all day, juggling childcare, the school run, and spreadsheets, and needed to get to the marsh to see some of the results of her hard work (at least, that is what I thought).

So after finishing with the last pole I drove home and executed my plan. Susanna was reluctant as she had a million things to do, but Colin (our current conservation science officer) was happy to watch the kids, and I insisted. We were rewarded with an enormous flock of Levant Sparrowhawks high in the sky. There were three or four hundred, like mosquitos dancing in a spiralling swarm trying to gain more height. Clearly they were not going to roost. But as the afternoon sun got lower, it was not long before one and then another, three and then six and soon scores of Lesser Spotted Eagles – black shapes on enormous rectangular wings – silently glided over our heads and settled in the trees close to where I had been labouring all day. We stared awestruck.

---

[27] NLT.

The sacred moment lingered but was then suddenly shattered as a single retort rang out from close to where the eagles had landed. I was running before the black crumpled shape hit the ground. The roosting raptors were in the air trying to gain height as quickly as possible with powerful but ponderous wing beats. A young man was reloading ready for another desecration. It would take me a minute or so to get to him.

I shouted, as loudly as I could, "Stop!"

The sound of my own heart pounding was in my ears, but as I ran over the tussocks and jumped the narrow ditches I did not hear another shot.

When I caught up with my quarry I saw there were two young men, neither armed, and both walking quickly away from where the eagle had fallen.

Between gasps I managed to accuse them: "You just shot an eagle!"

"No, we didn't – we heard the noise but we are just on a walk," said the older of the two; he looked about twenty-five.

I was bemused. There was no one else around and there was a dead eagle 100 yards away under the trees. I also noticed that there was something else on the ground. I picked up a gun.

"So this is not yours, then?" I asked, showing them the shotgun, worn and old but clearly still useable.

"No," they replied in unison.

"In that case, I will take it – we can't leave dangerous weapons out in the countryside, can we?"

Their faces gave away the anguish of their position. Keep to their story and they would lose the gun; admit it was theirs and they would be caught hunting an eagle and that would mean... Well, actually very little. I had no legal jurisdiction over them. I was on my own and the estate guards would take at least twenty minutes to get here if I called them on the cellphone. I would lecture them and they would leave. But they did not know all of that. What was so encouraging was that they felt ashamed – ashamed enough to lose their weapon, and unsure – unsure enough that they believed the consequences could be severe if caught illegally hunting in the wetland.

And I had a gun.

I put it in our storeroom and forgot all about it until a few months later when a somewhat abashed farmer came up to me one morning while I was working at the stable block on the estate.

"Good morning, Mr Chris," he started. "My name is Abu Amer. I am the father of Amer and Malik. I think you met them a few months ago."

I wracked my brain. I could not remember an Amer nor a Malik. I must have looked blank.

"I am very ashamed. They killed a great bird, an eagle, and you were there. You found the gun and took it."

"Oh, those two! Yes, I remember them. I have the gun but they swore it was not theirs."

"You were right to take it – you have every right to destroy it, but they have learned their lesson. They will never kill such birds again. I explained that it is *haram*, shameful to kill something so beautiful that you cannot even eat it. But the quail season will be here soon and they are game birds, legitimate to hunt. Will you give them back their gun?"

"I am here again tomorrow. If they come and explain what you have just said to me, they can have their gun."

They did come back and I occasionally met them hunting in the fields to the south far away from the estate and the wetland. I cannot be sure they only ever hunted game birds, but I am certain that they would never kill an eagle again.

CHAPTER 9

Crossing Cultures

2000
Jabal Rihan, Aammiq, Lebanon

I was in a wood with Abouna. The wood was high on the slopes of *Jabal* Rihan, the southern extension of Mount Lebanon, and Abouna was a Melkite priest who I had met in Beirut. He was trying to save the forested slopes above his ancestral village. Until very recently it would have been impossible to meet in this forest. The border with Israel was just a few miles away and the area had been part of the occupied zone until the troops had pulled out seven months before.

Conflict can be a strange bedfellow with conservation. Mostly, war is supremely destructive. Endangered habitats and wildlife suffer along with everything else. This was certainly our experience at Aammiq, where tens of thousands of trees were lost during the war years and destructive roads driven into the mountains. However, occasionally, war sets patches of habitat off-limits. People stay away and wildlife thrives. This woodland was one of those places.

"Don't step there!" shouted Abouna, as we entered the wood. "Only walk on the large rocks or in the paths of the Wild Boar."

"And why is that?" I asked, a cold feeling spreading through my chest as I had already guessed what would follow.

"Mines," he said, casually. "The whole area is mined, has been for years. Oh, and don't pick *anything* up."

"OK. So first things first," I responded, trying to keep the note of rising panic from my voice.

"Should we be here at all, and what have Wild Boar got to do with anything?"

"I thought that would be obvious," Abouna called over his shoulder as he hopped from one large flat rock to another.

He had found the track he was looking for and was now fast disappearing along a well-worn path, beaten level among the undergrowth. I could just make out what he was saying as he continued his explanation: "Wild Boar are heavy enough to set off any mines – so if we follow their paths we will be quite safe."

I couldn't fault his logic, nor his local knowledge, so to make sure I benefited from both, I quickly caught up. It was much easier than it seemed. The paths were wide, easy to spot, and very extensive, showing just how numerous the boar population had become.

"And why shouldn't I pick anything up?" I continued.

"Well, nothing man-made, particularly if it looks like a pack of sweets, biscuits, or cigarettes. The bombs in the area are packaged to look inviting – pick it up and boom! No more bird monitoring." Abouna explained it as if he were talking about the miniature cyclamen growing in profusion under the trees, or the delicate blue anemones poking their heads between the rocks.

So, I didn't pick up *anything*, and it wasn't just so that we could continue our birding. That was why I was here: to catalogue the birds and other wildlife of the forest. Abouna had gathered a flock of scientists to make an inventory of the wood so that he could make a presentation to the authorities; a catalogue of riches that had survived, against the odds, in this precious fragment and artefact of war. Most of the trees in the region had long been cleared, but the current threat to the habitat was no longer conflict but an explosion in development; a building boom. If the experience of Beirut was to be repeated, it would be in the post-war years that most of the natural habitat would be lost. In the dash for growth, regulations were often inadequate or ignored, and natural areas, soon to become urban sprawl, poorly understood and little studied. With concrete being the new habitat, wildlife literally went to the wall.

Abouna recognized that the population returning after the end of the Israeli occupation needed houses, schools, shops, and roads. But he also realized that they had been left a gift from previous generations. It had been locked in storage and was now unexpectedly precious and rare. With planning and care the communities could grow *and* preserve their natural heritage. The village could keep its backcloth of oak and pistachio, sycamore and myrtle, while housing its returning refugees and educating its children.

However, bringing a community to the point where it is prepared to limit its ambition, to put boundaries on its development, requires a long conversation. Our bird monitoring was providing some of the context for the discussion, but Abouna also took lessons from the community involvement at Aammiq. Increasingly we found this to be the case. Yes, we were often asked (and even occasionally paid) to study the wildlife of areas in need of conservation, to help assemble the scientific case for their protection, but even more often groups came to Aammiq to see how a community dialogues and decides to restrain itself from more and more consumption of land, resources, and wildlife to the benefit of all and for a heritage to be passed on to future generations.

One of the great things about being involved in a community dialogue is who you meet and who you enlist to help to bring the information to inform the decisions. A Rocha brought three things to the conversation at Aammiq.

Firstly, we recruited a stream of experts who could study the ecosystem of the wetland and answer such questions as: "What animals and plants live there? What do they need to thrive? How does the wetland work? Which parts are the most important for flood control, water retention and so on?"

Secondly, we helped the community experience the majesty and delight of creation. This happened in two places – certainly in the wetland with enthusiastic children catching tadpoles, overawed adults looking at the iridescent plumage of a kingfisher, and farmers learning about the microclimate the wetland created, benefiting their crops. But it also happened in churches where, with the congregations, we unpacked the Bible's message to look after, to steward, the creation. A favourite verse of mine to get discussion started was perhaps the best-known verse in the Bible "God so loved the... [cosmos] that he gave his one and only Son, that whoever believes in him shall not perish but have eternal life."[28] Just by using the original term from the Greek, "cosmos", rather than "world" immediately set preconceptions astir and got people to listen and talk.

Thirdly, we worked with the estate and community to implement the habitat protection and restoration project, overseeing ditches closed, pools created, dams constructed, trees planted, and a hundred other things that make up a community conservation project.

This is also a global conversation. The landowners, farmers, scientists, villagers, hikers, artists, and hunters of Aammiq are actors in microcosm. All over the world, communities are engaged in the same discussion. Because these issues cannot be confined to communal, local, national, or even regional borders, this is a truly global dialogue.

Unfortunately with global dialogues, rather than local ones, there is often a disconnect; those who are responsible for the greatest consumption are not the ones most aware of the destruction. So we can have our hardwood furniture without seeing the loss of Indonesia's forests, and the communities of the Maldives may lose their homes to sea-level rise without having contributed their fair share to the atmospheric carbon. Not so at the local level. Communities know the winners and losers in the race for consumption. "Consumption" and "consumers" are powerful terms that we hear every day. It doesn't seem strange so to self-identify, but if we pause for a moment, what an extraordinary way to think about ourselves! Bishop James Jones argues that to define ourselves in terms of what we eat, devour, and destroy is at odds with living on a planet with finite resources.[29]

---

[28] John 3:16, NIV, UK 2011.
[29] www.liverpool.anglican.org/Bishop-James-sets-out-sustainable-challenge (accessed 5.11.14).

Chris and Susanna with Samuel and Chloe just before they leave for the Middle East, 1994.

Qab Elias, the Bekaa Valley, Lebanon, 1996.

White Stork

Short-toed Eagle

Honey Buzzard

Black Stork

Tree Frog (*Hyla savignyi*)

Participants in the first bird identification training in Lebanon by A Rocha. Lake Qaraoun, the Bekaa Valley, 2002.

Our second Beirut neighbourhood, Menara 2008.

The Bekaa Valley in mist with the village of Saghbine in the foreground and Mount Hermon in the distance.

Young shepherds at work, the West Bekaa, Lebanon.

A well-earned tea break at a Bedouin encampment.

Aammiq wetland in winter looking south along the Mount Lebanon range.

The family at the archaeological site at Byblos shortly before we left Lebanon, Spring 2009.

Chris with Sam and Chloe at the Temple of Jupiter, with the Temple of Bacchus behind, Baalbek, 1998.

The Maronite Cathedral of St George with the Mohammed Al-Amin Mosque behind, Beirut.

The Aammiq wetland, summer 1997.

The Aammiq wetland after the conservation project, summer 2007.

Aammiq wetland looking west to the Barouk Ridge of the Mount Lebanon range.

The World Wildlife Fund has produced a really powerful way to think about all this. To help us put our consumption into planetary perspective, they have calculated that if everyone lived like X we would need Y planets to provide for our consumption, and deal with our waste. As a global community, we are living beyond our means by a factor of one and a half. As a Brit living in the UK with my fellow islanders we are living at a rate that would require three planet Earths if the whole human race had our collective lifestyle.[30]

But I digress. This is a story of a wetland and we were engaged in its conservation, in the beauty and tragedy of the Bekaa. Whether the rains would come and how hot the summer would be were to be played out at a global level, but whether we had a habitat to save or not was for the community of the West Bekaa.

From the very beginning, when the Harrises had asked us to lead the project, my greatest anxiety had been how on earth we would recruit the team with the wide range of skills needed to see the conservation of the wetland through. We needed, to name but a few: hydrologists, botanists, agriculturalists, educators, entomologists, and ornithologists, as well as water engineers, eco-tourism providers, and business strategists.

The answer came in the shape of the many different nationalities of team members, volunteers, and resident experts who gave extravagantly of their time, and for some whole chunks of their lives. Mostly our long-term team members were either locally employed or came as self-funded volunteers through the A Rocha network. We were supported by a host of experts drawn largely from fellow conservation NGOs that grew, while we were there, to be the backbone of the conservation movement in the country, supported by the Ministry of Environment and several university departments. To give some idea of the scale of global support, these are the nationalities of the team and long-term volunteers that worked with us through our time in the project: three from

---

[30] www.wwf.org.uk/what_we_do/about_us/building_a_one_planet_future.cfm (accessed 5.11.14).

the USA, seven Brits, four Canadians, one Dutch, two French, four Lebanese, one Palestinian, two Syrians, one Swiss, and a New Zealander, as well as other innumerable volunteers from all over the world.

They all added to the richness and the hard grind of cross-cultural working. I loved working with such a diverse group. Nevertheless, a cross-cultural team is hard work. Everyone comes with their own cultural presuppositions, except they don't see them as presuppositions at all. Each of us brings a set of norms, ways we see the world and ways we expect others to see it. These are products from our culture – comforting, normal, and shared; well, at least they are shared back home. The trouble with working outside your home country is that other cultures have their own presuppositions and they think they are normal too! With ever-increasing globalization, cross-cultural teams are more and more common, but mostly they don't operate as such. There is usually one dominant culture and that is most commonly the prevalent culture in situ. Those from outside this culture adapt and fit to the prevailing expectations and norms around them, and the team, although drawn from different nationalities, works in a mono-cultural way. This is easier, certainly, and often works very well, but it is not functionally cross- or even multicultural.

It wasn't like that for us. Usually there was not one dominant nationality, and even if there was it was never Lebanese, the cultural context where we all worked. It all led to a lot of discussion – trying to tease apart why Charbel had said that, and why Carol was so upset, and why the Lebanese schools were always late!

Time, punctuality, and lateness were certainly one of the default conflict zones; another was status. Different cultures can view status, how you get it, what it means, and how you can lose it, in quite different ways. Among some of our Lebanese team, we discovered a heightened sensitivity for the appropriateness of assignments given to particular team members that we rarely found with the more international set. An example might help here.

Richard and Yusef were in the middle of the wetland and they had a task to do. Richard was a PhD freshwater biologist from New Zealand and Yusef a recent biology graduate from a Beirut university. They were both team members, and in the heat of the late summer afternoon needed to take a sediment sample with an auger. An auger is like a great big apple corer that you screw into the ground and pull out, with several feet of sediment preserved in their depositional strata. It is hard, hot work and can take up to an hour a sample if the ground is hard. And today the ground was hard.

"Right, your turn," said Richard. "I think I got it down another foot."

Yusef took the auger and after a few ineffective turns flopped to the ground, angrily turning to Richard, saying, "This is ridiculous! We should not be doing this. It's too hot, and anyway we should employ a labourer for this sort of work. It's manual!" The last word was said as if it were a four-letter word.

Richard was completely confused. "But you said you were happy to help. You know we have to do it ourselves. I explained at the team meeting we can't employ anyone as it has to be done just so – otherwise the auger is likely to break off in the hard clay, and it's the only one we've got. This is what fieldwork is all about – it's great to be outside; just look around! What an amazing privilege to be out in a place like this and call it work. Where could possibly be better?"

Yusef's answer was heartfelt even if it was under his breath: "In an office with air-conditioning and a big desk!"

The soil sample was eventually taken, Richard doing 90 per cent of the work, but the incident led to a much greater understanding of Yusef's perspective as we talked about it afterwards. Yusef had recently graduated. He had a BSc. He and his parents had made great sacrifices so that he could get his degree. He did not sign up to the project for this. It was beneath him, and what is more, far below Richard, who was a doctor of science! Yusef was happy to study birds, water levels, plants – "study" being the operative word because that was a task that required respect. It was science. He had studied hard and had earned that right. He had not worked all those years so he could dig holes.

As a project, we had to learn to respect both the New Zealand pioneer spirit, complete with its zeal for the outdoors and enjoyment of manual labour, and the cultural appropriateness of tasks required of local staff. Although foreigners could happily ignore the messages given out by their activities, for a local team member, taking part in tasks that were seen as beneath them or demeaning had real consequences for their social standing, which understandably they were keen to preserve.

It is not a big jump from talking about status in the Middle East to a whole dialectic around the ideas of honour and shame often attributed to the region. The idea is that a man's (you will see why I say "man's" in a moment) position in society is maintained by the guarding of his honour, composed of his uprightness of character, his integrity, his glory, even. His store of honour can be added to by hard work and success in business, a moral and upstanding family, and by religious piety. But honour is a fragile thing and can easily be lost, particularly through the inappropriate sexual relations of his female family members.

The antithesis of honour is shame, and according to this analysis, women are in constant danger of losing their own honour and bringing shame on the family if they are compromised. This is often contrasted with a Western guilt culture. Here individuals act to reduce guilty feelings that are the consequence of behaviours considered "wrong", leading them to conformity. In honour cultures, the driving force is saving face and maintaining pride and honour in a societal context as opposed to keeping a clear conscience in a guilt culture.

There is no doubt these have been powerful tools in explaining different societies' methods of control and conformity. However, I recognized elements of both in the "Western" suburban semi-detached culture I grew up in and in the communities of the rural Bekaa Valley where we lived for many years. One of the great problems with the honour/shame discourse is the word "honour" itself. In the British mind (I will be specific here) it conjures up images of knights, jousting tournaments, castles, and a round table; in other words, an archaic world with little relevance to our own. By using the term so liberally we are in the greatest danger of Orientalism,[31] defining the "East", wherever that is, in contradiction and opposition to the "West" which we think we understand because we think it is "us", as if we were a unified group.

If you Google the words "Arab, honour and shame" you discover (as with most Google searches) an eclectic array of articles and posts. First, of course, comes Wikipedia, and then a varied assortment of blogs, news stories, and scholarly abstracts. The interesting thing for me was that I had to get to the forty-sixth search result before I found an Arab author. That article was a lone island in a sea of Western voices (it was an academic article critical of theoretical research). It is also interesting to note where these voices come from and why they have been written. In my Google search, articles number two, three, four, and six were from blogs and articles highly critical of Islam and the Arab world.

One of the real dangers of this external diagnosis is that it isn't long before peace prospects in the Middle East are raised within the dialectic and, hardly surprisingly, the honour/shame paradigm is seen as an elemental barrier within the Arab culture to meaningful negotiation.

These are serious consequences for an easy stereotyping. Said's masterly account of the dangers of this approach in his book *Orientalism* make startling reading. He defines Orientalism itself as "a kind of intellectual power", a "library or archive of information"… the archive is bound together by a family of ideas with a unifying set of values.[32] The problem is that the archive is built of generalizations made out of observable details, and these generalizations are elevated to immutable laws about the Orient, its nature, temperament,

---

[31] As defined in Edward Said's seminal book *Orientalism*, London: Penguin, 2003.
[32] Said, *Orientalism*, p. 41.

mentality, custom, and type.[33] This leads to a polarization – "the Oriental becomes more Oriental, the Westerner more Western",[34] which limits the human encounter between different cultures. And that is the danger.

Perhaps one area where a polarization has been magnified by the global media is the issue of "honour killings", that is, killings of female family members to preserve family honour. Honour killings are an atrocity and in some communities they are increasing. The Honour Based Violence Awareness Network estimates that there are around 5,000 honour killings globally a year, the largest numbers being from rural India and Pakistan with 1,000 each. There are an estimated 12 honour killings per year in the UK,[35] 20–30 in Jordan, 200–300 in Syria and 400 in Yemen.[36] These are horrifying statistics and if all 5,000 are the result of Muslim family murder they represent a figure of 3.2 per million Muslim women murdered by their families annually. Equally horrifying are the statistics for American women and girls murdered by their own families, which in 2008 numbered some 930. As a percentage of the population, that comes out an equally alarming 3.1 per million American women and girls murdered by their families annually.[37]

Although a sad feature of some communities in the region, as these figures show, it is rare, and in Lebanon only one family we knew were touched by this horror. For them it was quite different to the usual stereotype.

I had got to know Aadil and his quiet wife Saleema in the saddest of circumstances. I had just finished my weekly circuit of the wetland and was walking back to the car, parked on one of the agricultural tracks that led to the avenue of trees and the Riachi River that bordered the wetland to the south. It was August, so I

---

[33] Said, *Orientalism*, p. 86.

[34] Said, *Orientalism*, p. 46.

[35] http://hbv-awareness.com/ (accessed 5.11.14).

[36] http://wikiislam.net/wiki/Muslim_Statistics_-_Honor_Violence (accessed 5.11.14).

[37] www.examiner.com/article/honor-killings-lies-damn-lies-and-statistics (accessed 5.11.14).

had set off late and knew that other than the arriving Hoopoes, the earliest of the migrants, there would not be much stirring in the wetland as the heat baked the landscape biscuit-dry.

I passed the small Bedouin camp in the shade of the trees, a ragtag collection of a couple of tents and stockades built for the temporary safety of their goats. A tall, thin, and shy-looking man, reminding me of an earnest sixth-former, asked that I stop by his tent for coffee. I was happy to oblige; the tent would be cool, the coffee good, and the hospitality genuine. On entering I could tell something was wrong. A young woman was lying, breathing quietly, on her bed while Aadil poured me the coffee, already made and hot on the coals. After thanking him and taking a sip of the bittersweet nectar I asked if his wife was all right.

Matter of factly he explained that she had given birth last night to a baby here in the tent. The labour was difficult, Aadil's mother-in-law was unable to save the child, and so he died. They had buried the baby boy under the large tree by the river. In the morning, Aadil had walked to the nearby village and brought a doctor who, bringing Aadil back by car, had checked his wife and given her some pills. The doctor had said Saleema would be fine but they needed to get the prescription the doctor had left, so would I take Aadil to Qab Elias, so he could go to the pharmacy and collect the medicine?

"Of course! We can go right away, but why didn't you take Saleema to the hospital last night?" I asked, clumsily.

Aadil was patient as he explained: "We don't have a car. Labour started at two in the morning. It would take me an hour to walk to the road and longer to hail a passing car. They wouldn't drive here anyway, and we can't afford the hospital."

In silent shock I drove Aadil to Qab Elias and brought him back to Saleema, who was under the loving care of her mother when we returned. I checked up on the couple each morning after that and soon, as the doctor had promised, Saleema was up and about, well in body but grieving inside the dark of her tent cocoon.

151

I expected the couple to be in their lonely but beautiful setting for the autumn, as that was usually the custom, leaving when the rains brought life to other areas of the Bekaa not blessed by the wetland. So I was greatly surprised when, early one morning in October, the tent was gone. Evidence of their camp was all around as the flotsam and jetsam of their lives clung to the thorn bushes beyond the manicured stubble that the goats had consumed in the field that served for grazing. I hurried to the car and back to *Houch Aammiq* to see if anyone knew why the family, together with the flocks, had gone so suddenly.

I joined Hana, one of the farmhands, and the group of gathering labourers who were arriving, drawn by the rumours they had heard. Hana, wizened and toothless, hailed from somewhere close to the Euphrates in Syria. I found his accent hard to follow at the best of times. With an audience and centre stage he became dramatic and incomprehensible, at least to me. Faaris translated.

Saleema's uncle had turned up late the previous evening. From Hana's hand gestures he was clearly a bad man and, by the grumbles that erupted on his entry to the story, disliked by the assembled labourers who knew him or of him. After the angry chatter died down, Hana continued. The uncle had been drinking, and he bragged that he was not scared of Aadil, and that he would go and see his niece if he wanted to.

At this point I realized there was common knowledge that I lacked, as no one seemed surprised that the uncle was unlikely to receive a friendly welcome at the small camp. Despite Hana's sage advice, the uncle did walk to the camp. When he arrived, Aadil promptly entered his tent, returning a few seconds later with a loaded revolver. I assumed Hana must have accompanied the uncle to provide us with the details. Aadil simply said, "You should not have come back" and shot him dead.

All in attendance agreed that this was a fair end to the feud, for that is what it had been. The feud had started when the uncle forced himself on Saleema years before. Aadil had sworn to avenge his young wife's honour and the uncle had fled, to foolishly return.

CHAPTER 10

The Day the World Changed

2001
Clemenceau, Beirut

We were surrounded by packing cases and plastic-wrapped furniture but we were in! We had made the move from the Bekaa to Beirut. It seemed as if we should have shown our passports at the mountain checkpoint as this was a different country, a different world. Our flat was on the sixth floor of a family-owned apartment block, with the family business taking up the first two floors. The sea was less than a mile away, but despite the fact that the ground rose steeply from the seaside promenade, we could only catch a glimpse of the Mediterranean sparkling between the shopping precincts, banks, and office blocks scraping the skyline.

This was our fourth move as, after the "lovely ugly house" we spent a year in Zahle, the Hakim family having eventually sold the property. But this move would be quite different. We had finally lost the battle to educate the children in the Bekaa. Of course tens of thousands of children are schooled in the valley and go on to thrive at university and in employment at home and abroad. But we had the problem of the expat, made more extreme as we were almost the only foreigners. Fundamentally it was a problem of language. There is a myth that if you bring kids up in a country with a different language to their native tongue they will become bilingual;

the truth is that some will and some won't. It depends on a number of factors, including the language of the formal education and of their friendship groups. Sam and Chloe had mostly been taught in English but operated in Arabic and English in the playground. This meant that the English medium subjects were accessible to them but their Arabic wasn't up to learning the others. That was part of the problem.

The other side of the story was that the new "American branded" school where they had been taught for several years was having great difficulty recruiting qualified English-speaking staff. To our horror we discovered that Sam, at the grand age of ten, was often used to teach the lesson to his classmates as his English was better than the teacher's. Some staff were inhibited by having fluent English speakers in the class and so took it out on our kids – resorting to corporal punishment to prop up their dignity. It was time to put the kids in an international school in Beirut.

We had been planning the move for months. We secured three places in the new school; we found an apartment in the city and arranged for a new way of working for the team. The idea had been that I would make the inverse commute from the capital to the countryside a couple of days a week, while the children could walk to the American Community School in Beirut in the central district of Hamra. The work at the wetland could continue as Andy and Laurel were now based in the village of Aana close by, where we had set up an office and guest house. As well as running the visitor and volunteer programme, they were busy with field research and a thriving school and university programme that we operated from a classroom created from an old stable and storage room at *Houch Aammiq*.

My work had been increasingly taking me to Beirut for meetings with other conservation NGOs, universities and government departments, and so it seemed to matter less that we lived close to the wetland, particularly as we left the work in such capable hands.

As we gazed at our new neighbourhood in the late afternoon September sun, the phone rang.

"There has been a bomb!" announced Laurel, our Canadian colleague who, with her American husband, Andy, was now heading up the team in the Bekaa.

It was the news we were always waiting for, and Susanna went into a well-practised drill. "Are you both OK? Where was the bomb? Do you need to leave the Bekaa?"

"It was a plane! It flew into the Trade Center… it's awful. We have had family phoning us non-stop. They say we should come home. We have had a steady stream of neighbours arriving telling us it isn't safe to stay. Americans are the target," Laurel continued breathlessly.

Susanna was confused. "What? Where was the plane? What has happened?"

"A plane has been flown into the World Trade Center in New York. Hundreds are dead. The towers are down."

"We haven't heard anything. We haven't tuned in the TV. But if it is in the US, it is best to stay where you are," Susanna said, trying to exude calm over the phone.

"Perhaps for now, but hundreds of Americans are dead and there are Palestinian refugees in their Lebanese camps handing out sweets, celebrating."

"Listen," said Susanna. "Just stay in the village. You are well known there and quite safe. We will try to find out what is going on and get back to you."

I went down to join Ahsraf the *natur*, the caretaker of the apartment block, a Coptic Christian, with his friends, the fellow *naturs* of the surrounding buildings. They were glued to the TV, silent and shocked.

"Have you seen the news?" asked Ashraf.

"No, but we heard something has happened in New York. We don't have a working TV. Can I watch with you?"

As the footage was repeated again and again, the impact, the cloud of smoke, the collapse of the towers, the true horror sank in and with it the realization that life would never be quite the same again for us and many, many others.

"I heard that some people in Lebanon have been celebrating. Is it true? Has there been anything in the news?" I asked.

Yusef, a Palestinian eking out a meagre existence in the basement of the next-door block, cleared his throat to speak. "Yes, some people in the camps have been celebrating. They hope that this day has changed the world. America knows what it is like now. America has joined our world: perhaps that will change it for everyone."

"We have Americans in a village in the Bekaa. Do you think they are safe?" I asked, getting to the question uppermost in my mind.

I had spent time with this group during the days when we were looking for an apartment in the area, so they knew of the project and why there were foreign volunteers in the Bekaa.

"Yes, they will be fine in the village; they have been taken to its heart, they are part of the community. But who knows what will happen outside? The world has changed," Ashraf predicted.

Our plans had seemed so sensible, but that was before 11 September. Now was it safe for Andy and Laurel to stay? How would the US respond? Would there be more terrorist outrages? What would it mean for the region? Would it change local attitudes to Westerners? Would we become targets?

Andy and Laurel returned to the States, attending the wedding of friends, and extended their leave, giving us time to watch and wait for some answers. The whole world watched and listened as the rhetoric became more and more bellicose, the diplomacy, by some, more desperate – and the region slid slowly but inexorably to war.

It took a full twenty-one months, but all of our friends and neighbours were confident that war was coming from the earliest days. We dissected news reports, followed the intricacies of weapons inspections, UN mandates, and sanctions. We listened carefully to advice from the British and American embassies and had long conversations with members of the A Rocha Lebanon board of trustees that had been formed to guide the project in its early years. Certainly it didn't help the case for Andy and Laurel to stay that one of the suicide pilots of the 9/11 attacks grew up less than ten miles from Aammiq and the village where the team was based.[38]

Ironically, as question marks grew over the viability of a foreign team in the Bekaa, we were entering a period of unparalleled opportunity. Increasingly we were working with other conservation NGOs. Across the country, local groups and national organizations were battling to protect Lebanon's dwindling wildlife from rapid development, pollution, and hunting. Our work at Aammiq had become well known and our local collaboration with the neighbouring Al Shouf Cedar Nature Reserve was extended to include groups protecting forests, coasts, rivers, and mountain sites. As we became more and more engaged in the national conservation movement, we realized a key bottleneck to better protection of birds was the chronic lack of trained researchers who could reliably identify birds to a species level. To address this, we developed a training course covering bird identification, behaviour, migration and conservation – "Birds 101".

Andy, our ornithologist, was writing the course and would deliver it. As the clouds of war continued to build, Andy and Laurel returned to Lebanon. He had written an extraordinary course and we assembled the first-ever bird identification training programme for a dozen or so of Lebanon's front-line defenders of biodiversity.

While we were learning how to tell the difference between flocks of storks, cranes, and pelicans from the grace of their outlines across the sky, the world continued its focus on squadrons of a very different kind. The talk was all of rockets, missiles, chemical and biological weapons, and whether they were stockpiled in the deserts of Iraq. Although the war was still a year away, the tension was palpable and it became untenable to leave Andy and Laurel living in the valley. They were known and loved by friends and neighbours, but they were the only expat American citizens in a very wide radius. If some unknown group or individuals had wanted to vent

---

[38] www.pbs.org/wgbh/pages/frontline/shows/network/personal/whowere.html (accessed 5.11.14).

their fury or grab the headlines, shooting Andy would be an easy way to do it. So it was with very heavy hearts that we said goodbye as they relocated back to the US; a small detail in the catalogue of consequences from the build-up to the Second Gulf War.

With a reduced team and the threat of regional conflict hanging over us, we stopped receiving international visitors and volunteers. I spent rather more of my time on the Beirut to Bekaa highway than had been planned, but the work at Aammiq continued to thrive. After such a long gestation, the war storm when it broke was shockingly powerful. It burst with the bombing of Baghdad and once again we were watching scenes of shock and awe played over streets we had got to know and neighbourhoods that we had visited.

Universally our friends and neighbours had told us, after the shock of 9/11 had worn off, that the US and allies would declare war on Iraq. They expected it, they knew it was coming, and they were angry. They had little time for Saddam Hussein. They thought him a monster and his regime repugnant but they feared what would replace it. They also deeply resented the "meddling" of Western powers and predicted that in the long run, a second Iraq war would make the region less stable. Perhaps more than anything else, however, there was a deep sense of resentment that the world was being presented with such a binary choice: "You are with us or against us, on the side of good or part of the axis of evil."

For the most part their identity lay in neither option, but they would feel the consequences of decisions made in Washington and Baghdad, London and Brussels, more keenly than most.

And what of the response from our neighbours, colleagues, villagers, farmers, and friends to citizens of the countries that were now bombing a fellow country member of the Arab League? Mostly, they made a very clear distinction between people and their government's foreign policy. Almost all decried the British and American intervention, but they treated us in just the same way that they always had; as friends, colleagues, and neighbours. There was no way that they would like to have been tarred with the same brush as previous Lebanese administrations, and certainly did not think we bore any responsibility for our governments' actions.

It was probably hardest for the children. The school offered European, American, and Lebanese curricula. Perhaps a third of the teachers were expats and many of the children had foreign passports. However, they were nearly universally from international Lebanese families with deep roots in the region. The number of students with only one foreign passport was tiny. School playgrounds can be very tough places and Chloe, particularly at the tender age of ten, had to contend with significant nationalistic feeling and abuse, particularly when the 24-hour news flashed scenes of human carnage over the nation's TV screens. However, the children were able to navigate their own social minefields partly because, ironically, they understood Lebanon more fully than many of their classmates of the international Lebanese set. On one particular occasion, in Sam's class, the children were surveyed as to how long they had lived in Lebanon. Sam, the only non-Lebanese, had lived in the country the longest and a full two years ahead of the closest contender.

In the midst of these epoch-changing times, we were getting to know our new neighbourhood. A favourite family walk along the seaside Corniche revealed the diversity of our new neighbours, giving a very different flavour depending on the season and time of day the walk was taken. We particularly loved the wide pavement, set a few metres above the rocky shore, in winter just after a storm. The promenade would be mostly empty as huge waves would crash onto the sea wall, the platform for the pavement, occasionally breaking over the railings to soak the shrieking teenagers playing chicken with the sea. As the water flooded onto the carriageway of the road, the laughing youngsters would reassemble to take selfies with their cellphones, the next wave coming to soak them in the background. Determined keep-fit enthusiasts bedecked in waterproofs would swerve round the puddles as they kept to their rhythm, fighting the pounds, and bored Sri Lankan and Filipina maids would wait patiently while the dogs they were walking relieved themselves against the palm trees.

If the sea came to life in the winter, the Corniche came to life in the summer. In the early morning, joggers would be making the most of the coolest part of the day. Some were dressed in the latest keep-fit fashion, but others donned the same waterproofs as if it were still winter and rain a possibility. They weren't protecting themselves from getting wet but forcing their bodies to sweat away the weight. As the heat of the day built up, the shore was taken over by the boys. At the weekend every flat rock was festooned with tanning male bodies and where the raised pavement ran alongside the deepest pools, the balustrade would become an impromptu diving platform, a catwalk of muscle waiting in line. Very occasionally a family group would stake out a pitch on one of the few sections of shingle beach. The men would swim and dive, wearing only swimming shorts, but the girls would enter the water in full *abiyah*, wading into the bath-warm water of the larger rock pools in their flowing personal tents.

But it was at night that the Corniche belonged to the families. As it grew dark, cars would park on the kerbside under the palm trees of the central reservation and pack the side streets leading down to the sea. Whole families, three generations rich, would emerge from old battered saloons and modern SUVs and set up station on the asphalt. Swathed in diaphanous black, aged grandmothers would sit on folding chairs while the younger women tried to feed reluctant toddlers who would rather run or, better still, play with the brightly coloured toys on offer from a covey of hawkers selling the latest plastic fads from China. Courting couples, heavily chaperoned, promenaded, competing with chains of girls, arms linked, who took up half the pavement as they meandered through the gathering crowds. And, of course, there were the *shabaab*, the young men, peacock-preening, in small groups under the street lamps or listening to the music blasting from their car stereos, their gift to the party.

As well as the drumbeat, heavy scents filled the air, rising from the carts stationed every 100 yards or so along the entire length of the street. There was corn on the cob hissing on the barbeque, hot candied nuts cemented in sugar brittles or loose and covered with toffee and sesame seeds, shockingly pink and stickily sweet *chaer binaat*, girls' hair,[39] and hot salted chickpeas spiced with lemon. Darting between customers, the *kahwajis* advertised their cardamom-spiked coffee by clicking two tiny coffee cups together, castanet-style, as if the smell of the freshly roasted beans was not enough to ensure sales.

We always felt welcome at these evening festivities, although as the international rhetoric intensified and the slide to war gathered momentum, the urban art and graffiti took a menacing tone. The image of the falling bomb was oft-repeated on posters and handbills, their colour schemes starkly black and white with intrusions of slashing red. Western political figures, caricatured and grotesque, were shown as puppet masters or chess players rearranging the region to suit their own ends, but no one singled us out for blame.

The only violence that was directed at me during this period had nothing to do with the Gulf War or with my being a Brit and so a citizen of one of the countries fighting in Iraq. I was in Sin el Fil, an area of Beirut that I did not know well. I was looking for a particular office. I had the address, but addresses could be a mixed blessing in Beirut. The official names for roads were rarely used. Often there was a popular street name that had no relation to anything on the rare maps that you could find in those days, and few buildings were numbered. Navigation was done by way of landmarks and by frequently stopping to ask pedestrians the way. The only problem with this strategy was that there was a deep reluctance to admit you might not know the whereabouts of the requested destination. Therefore, everyone you stopped to ask had an opinion, and many of them were contradictory.

While I was in this confused state I must have stood out as an easy target. In any event I felt a mild brush past me and a ruffle

[39] Or, as it is known in the UK, candyfloss.

in my jacket pocket. Realizing that my wallet was about to go, I whipped round to catch the pickpocket. The next thing I knew I was on the ground as my twist had been halted by a stunning blow to the back of the head. Fury built and, picking myself off the ground, I saw the coat-tails of my assailant disappear down a side street 50 yards or so ahead. I took chase. I had no chance of catching him. I was winded, and he had a head start and knew the maze of side streets and alleyways that made up this part of town. I paused to catch my breath at the junction, pondering what to do next. In the event, any decision was going to be taken by the crowd of enraged men gathered around me.

"Are you OK?" asked the nearest suited gentleman. "I saw what happened. It's appalling. In our streets, too! This is a good neighbourhood."

"We can get him," chimed in a second, younger man. His designer stubble, sunglasses, and upturned collar made him look like he had just stepped from one of the fashion adverts lining the street. "I saw where he went."

Like an electric charge short-circuiting through the group, the spark ignited this collection of strangers into action. Growing by the second, rapid-fire Arabic gave direction to the energy and the posse was off, running in the direction of the culprit. I followed rather more slowly and stiffly. My ribs had taken a knock that I was only now becoming aware of, as the adrenalin subsided and curiosity took over: "What if they really find the thief? What will they do to him?"

As I looked down the side road, I could see the vigilantes searching the alleys, small shops, and numerous garages that were open to the street. It was in one of these that they caught the offender. He was young, perhaps nineteen or twenty, and terrified as he was dragged before me, his arms pinned, vice-like, to his sides by the burliest of the street protectors.

The well-dressed gentleman who had expressed the initial outrage had clearly become the leader of the group. He had my wallet held lightly in his perfectly manicured hand. Handing it to me, he asked for clarification of guilt: "Is this yours?"

Of course it was, as already attested to by the photo ID. Other than my cards it was, however, empty.

"Give him the money!" demanded the larger of the two handlers, while his partner squeezed his grip even tighter.

Despite his desperate situation, the pickpocket was clearly reluctant to part with his ill-gotten gains, which was understandable. I, like everyone else, carried the week's spending money in cash. So it was quite a wad of bills that was thrown at my feet as his guards started to shake him as if the Lebanese lira and dollar bills would fall from him like leaves from a tree in an autumn gale.

"Is it all there?" asked the fashionable young man. I counted the cash; it was.

"He is Egyptian, not Lebanese!" spat one of his assailants. "We found him in a garage. He is clearly living there, from all his trash, preying on good folk like you in our neighbourhood. Not any more."

"So what do you want us to do with him?" asked the self-appointed leader.

I was completely lost for words. Maybe it was the shock of the fall, but more likely it was the responsibility of having to decide the fate of the criminal moments after the crime.

Sensing my inability to even pull two thoughts together, let alone pass judgment and sentence on my attacker, the urbane city gent helpfully outlined my options: "We could take him to the police. They will rough him up and then he will spend months in a stinking hole of a prison, or we could beat him up and make sure he leaves the neighbourhood. Well, he will do that anyway, as we all know his face, where he lives, and what he does for a living now!"

"Don't take him to the police." I said instinctively. We had heard many stories of the police and what went on at some of the police stations. "I wouldn't wish that on anyone. But no, don't beat him up either. That would be terrible. Look, he has learned his lesson, and as you say, he won't do it again here. Beating him up won't make any difference. Let him go."

It was like a weight falling from my shoulders; the power of retribution on a victim is a heady thing.

Although a number of the encircled men looked disappointed, it was clearly totally up to me and so they let him go. He shot down the road like a rabbit released from a snare and my protectors drifted away as if they had done nothing more unusual than pause for a coffee in a local café. I thanked the dissipating group profusely. Mostly I just received nods of acknowledgment but one comment cut me to the quick.

"It is nothing. You and your fellow Brits would do just the same for any of us if we were in London and the same happened there."

CHAPTER 11

Myths, Legends, and Superstitions

2002–07
Tyre, Machnaqa, Afqa, Akkar-Donnieh, Lebanon

From the very early days of the conservation project, we realized that we had both a huge problem and a great opportunity. From a glass half-empty perspective, there were massive gaps in understanding the natural history of modern-day Lebanon. Looking at the glass as half-full, there was so much to be discovered! Along with one or two local team members, many of our international volunteers and staff were extraordinarily able birdwatchers and general all-round nature buffs. Folk such as Colin Beale, Rich Prior, Helen Demopolous, Colin Conroy, and Andy Sprenger really knew their birds and, in their own country contexts, had impressive life lists of species seen. Here was a country where new species could be added not just to personal but to the national list, flowers thought extinct rediscovered, and where first-ever breeding records were waiting to be catalogued. To give an idea of the excitement for the birding contingent of the team, these are the significant national records from the start of the project to 2008 made by the A Rocha team (you probably need to be a birder to use the word "excitement" in that last sentence):

- Greylag Goose 2000 first record
- Mallard, breeding for first time ever, 2005
- Garganey, breeding for first time ever, 1999, second time 2005
- Black Stork, first-ever wintering records, 2006 and 2007
- Marsh Harrier, breeding for first time ever, 2006
- Lesser Spotted Eagle, first-ever summering birds, 2001 and 2006
- Eurasian Eagle Owl, first confirmed breeding, 2004
- Long-eared Owl, first reconfirmed breeding (since Canon H. B. Tristram in 1864), 2006
- Oriental Crow *Corvus (corone) orientalis*, first record
- Bar-tailed Lark, first record 2000, first breeding proved 2005
- Desert Lark, first-ever breeding, 2006
- Scrub Warbler, first-ever breeding, 2006
- Greenish Warbler, first record, 2000
- Bearded Reedling, first record, 1996
- Black-throated Thrush, first record, 2000
- Desert Finch, first-ever summer record, singing male, 2006
- Little Bunting, first living sightings, 2003 (only previous record a specimen collected by Tristram in 1885)[40]

The list does not include the many other contributions, particularly changes of assumed status of species, for example, Temminck's Lark from vagrant to common breeder, nor the two new plant species and the confirmation of the Jungle Cat in the wetland

---

[40] Personal communication.

– a predator the size of a slim German shepherd dog that was unknown to the scientific community until the regular monitoring at the wetland.

In our conservation of the wetland we were concentrating on protecting and restoring habitats, and some of these national records were a result of such improvements for wildlife. New records were always exciting, and encouraged us all in the work we were doing. However, at a national level the fact that there were such significant gaps in understanding the nation's biodiversity made conserving it very difficult. Questions such as which routes do the migrating birds take while passing, twice a year, through the country were essential to answer. Without knowing the routes of these fly ways, how could the birds be protected?

To answer this and other questions, we developed an ambitious project with Lebanon's Birdlife International partner – the Society for the Protection of Nature in Lebanon (SPNL). Our idea was to survey the entire country for sites that met strict international criteria to be designated Important Bird Areas (IBAs).[41] These sites would be the sites harbouring the hundreds and thousands of eagles, buzzards, hawks, cranes, and pelicans on their migration odysseys. They would also be the sites with important breeding populations of regional specialties such as the Syrian Serin and Masked Shrike. It would take us four years and thousands of field hours of trekking through woodlands, walking along mountain ridges, staring through telescopes, and poring over identification books, but it also got the team to some completely new areas of Lebanon and the privilege of sharing with communities passionate about protecting their forest, their wetland, their birds, their animals, and plants.

One of the prospective sites for IBA status was the Tyre Coast Nature Reserve. Partly through the IBA programme, but also to support the government scheme to protect the rare dune system, I had the joy of travelling down the coast a couple of hours from Beirut to survey the site for birdlife. Unusually for the Lebanese

---

[41] www.birdlife.org/datazone/sowb/casestudy/80 (accessed 5.11.14).

coast, the beach at Tyre was a sweep of glorious golden sand. Beyond the usual tourist umbrellas, snack stands and makeshift car parks, the beach narrowed, fringing an undulating dune system of metal-green tussock and salt-tolerant plants. The dunes made up half of the significant habitat on the reserve, while the other half was comprised of small agricultural plots and wetlands overflowing from the freshwater springs at the inevitably named *Ras el Ain* (head of the spring). Between the two lived 31,478 Palestinian refugees in the Rashidiye refugee camp.[42]

It was a cool April morning, and as the sun played hopscotch with the scudding clouds I was at *Ras el Ain*, sitting on a carved Roman block, noting down the birds that came to the open pool, part of the ancient watercourse that had been channelled there for millennia. Distracted by a Little Bittern doing its best to remain invisible in the reeds at the back of the pool, I did not notice the figure making his way up the path, almost blocked with the runaway spring green of the Crown Daises and Chamomile, yellow and white heads tossing in the breeze.

"Can I have that – if you've finished with it?" asked the young man, perhaps twenty years old, pointing in the general direction of a can of Coke and the remains of my sandwich lunch.

Unsure quite what he wanted, I replied, "Um, I am afraid I have finished the Coke. If you are thirsty, I have some water in my bag."

"No, just the empty can, if you are finished."

It was only at that point that I saw the large plastic sack half-full with compressed soda cans at his feet.

After gratefully taking some of my rubbish, Fouad also accepted a drink and one of my sandwiches, and we sat talking.

"How long has it taken you to collect the cans in the bag?" I asked.

"A couple of hours," replied Fouad. "It is much easier in the summer. I go along the beach and clean up after the tourists; you can get three bags-full in an afternoon. But at this time of the year it is better to walk along the road or along the paths."

---

[42] www.unrwa.org/where-we-work/lebanon/camp-profiles?field=15 (accessed 5.11.14).

"How much do you get for the cans?"

"Each can is worth about a cent."

I did the maths – Fouad had worked for two hours and had collected, at most, fifty cans – so he brought in about twenty-five cents an hour.

Fouad knew what I was thinking.

"Not much, eh? But what else can I do? I'm Palestinian. I live in the camp. This is all I can do."

He said it with a deep resignation, but there was anger there too. Not directed at me, but just under the surface and raw.

Without any more prompting, his story poured out.

"I am the eldest of four brothers and one sister. With my parents and grandparents we live in an 80 square metre house – that's nine of us in a box. My father is sick; he can't work. Thanks be to God for UNRWA.[43] They treat him at the clinic and give us some help, occasionally. But mostly it is up to me and my brothers. Ahmad is working in a garage in the camp – he is really good with motorbikes. The rest of us work in the fields when we can – and when there is no work we collect cans for scrap."

"Where did your family come from?" I asked.

"Deir el Qassi is my family's village, it is in northern Palestine. My grandfather fled with the family during the *Nakba*.[44] My father was a baby. He is now sixty. He has been a refugee all his life."

I could sense that the same question was forming in Fouad's mind even as it formed in my own. Would he be a refugee all his life, too?

Suddenly Fouad changed the subject. He had told this stranger enough.

"What are you doing?"

Conscious that my work, just like my story, was so much easier than his, it seemed mildly ridiculous to recount the details of the IBA programme and the survey I was conducting of the freshwater ponds on the reserve.

---

[43] The *United Nations Relief and Works Agency* for Palestine refugees in the Near East.
[44] The Arabic term for the flight of Palestinians from their homes in 1948. Literally it means "disaster" or "catastrophe".

"But that's amazing! I love the birds that come here. My favourite are the pelicans that fly along the coast in the spring and autumn. Like bomber aircraft, they look too heavy to stay above the waves. The only good thing about this camp is that it is near the sea. When I just can't take the noise, the crowds and the smell any longer, I come here or I walk along the beach thanking God for the beauty of the sky and the ocean, a tiny bird in the trees, or the *rahu*."[45]

After Fouad had gone, looking for more cans to feed the family, I walked down to the shore. Between the springs and the beach it was a profusion of green. The handkerchief fields were groaning with fava beans and salad, the criss-crossing pathways punctuated poppy-red and the fallow ground a riot of field gladioli, pink flax and pimpernel. My mind wandered to a legend inspired perhaps by these very fields.

The Roman poet Ovid adds the detail to an already ancient myth that Zeus fell in love with a princess of Tyre. She was named centuries before as Europa, Europe's founding myth in the oldest surviving work of Greek literature – Homer's *Iliad*.[46] Along with her girlfriends she was enjoying the flower-filled meadows by the sea when Zeus, disguised as a majestic young bull, mingled with the grazing herd and beguiled the maidens with his magnificent form. Europa was entranced and climbed onto the animal's lithe back, only to be carried away to the island of Crete to found the Minoan race with none other than the father of the Greek pantheon. With decades of Western imperialism pushing ideas east, it is good to remember that for millennia most of the thought traffic had been in the opposite direction.

I was confronted again with the echoes of that westward flow of culture in the hills above Jounieh and Jbail at the sites around the Ibrahim River, redolent with ancient myths from the East, another setting for the IBA fieldwork in the mountains of Kesrouan.

---

[45] Common term used for great flocks of pelicans, storks, or other large birds on migration.

[46] Simon Price and Peter Thonemann, *The Birth of Classical Europe*, London: Penguin, 2011, p. 3.

From preparatory fieldwork we knew that at least in the autumn, a major route for soaring birds on their passage from Eastern Europe to Africa was some 20 to 30 km inland from the coast. By use of this route, the birds could avoid the Mediterranean while minimizing the flying distance travelled.[47] This meant that the corrugated country rising to the high peaks of Mount Lebanon on the nation's western side was a priority for fieldwork.

Frank and Laure Skeels in their book *Highways and Byways of Lebanon* describe the country as a "pleated skirt". In the foreword to their book they say that their "intention in writing this book was to show off The Lebanon to you and that is best done from a hilltop".[48] We took much the same approach to monitoring the birds, stationing ourselves on strategic hilltops to observe and record the flocks as they passed overhead. In taking up these positions for glorious, but neck-wrenching work, we followed the ancients and learned something of the myths of this convoluted landscape.

I had been to Machnaqa several times through the year to put in the fieldwork hours to generate the data we needed for the survey, but it was only when we went as a family for a picnic and to gather data on the vegetation that we discovered echoes of an older time. Susanna was by now busy working part-time for the children's school, to help reduce the never-ending grind of finding school fees, and part-time as accountant and office manager for the A Rocha project. With the move to Beirut we set up an office in the house to cope with the increasing paperwork that the national programmes generated. As well as the IBA project, we were working in schools, universities, and churches nationwide, and Susanna was the mainstay of keeping the finances and reporting in order.

With so much going on and part of our dining room being the centre of operations, we needed to find ways to preserve family

---

[47] "Autumn routes of migrating raptors and other soaring birds in Lebanon", *Sandgrouse* 23 (2) 2001, the magazine of the Ornithological Society of the Middle East.

[48] Frank and Laure Skeels, *A Comprehensive Guide Highways and Byways of Lebanon*, Reading, Berkshire: Garnet Publishing, 2001, p. x.

space. One way was to use the predictably glorious summer weather to be out and about exploring at the weekends. Work often snuck in to the family plans.

"It's gorgeous!" said Susanna, looking at the four pillars with their screen wall, the restored remnant of the ancient temple rising from the fine dressed stones tracing the outlines of a long-collapsed hypostyle, fallen as if it had grown and then died on the hilltop.

"I told you that you would like it. And look at the view!"

The hill afforded an excellent vantage point to watch the birds and enjoy the landscape. We used a limestone slab, the vine motif still just visible despite millennia of weathering, as a picnic table, and soaked up the sunshine and the views. All around, the temple lay in ruins, scattered as if a child, frustrated after hours of creative play, had destroyed their game, leaving the clearing-up for another day. Fragile pillars broken like candles lay in sections under the fading glory of the late summer maquis. Only the claret-red hollyhock and sulphur cistus brightened the long-dead undergrowth, sallow in the sun. Swallowtail butterflies drifted somnolently from stone to stone when disturbed from their stupor by the emerald flashes of the scaly lizards, energized by the heat.

Susanna and I wanted nothing more than to doze in the sun, joining the butterflies in their siesta. But the kids would have none of it. Armed with sticks, in the fashion of children everywhere, they marched as Romans, three abreast, a diminutive legion re-enacting an ancient clash of armies as they defended their hilltop redoubt. But it wasn't long before their manoeuvres led them to discoveries.

"Mum, Dad, come and look! Look what we've found."

They had discovered sarcophagi, a narrow rock passage, and a tortoise. After counting the rings on the scales of the reptile to estimate its age (a healthy ten-year-old specimen), we tried to decipher the ancient art. All was blurred, myopia brought on by centuries of weather, but two figures stood out from an indistinct crowd: a man with an arm extended, and a seated woman weeping. The children's competing interpretations became more and more fanciful in this passageway to the dead and so, for more scholarly theories, we turned to our guidebook to make sense of the dying echoes of this antique landscape. We discovered that we were sitting at the halfway point on a pilgrimage that followed the river from the sea to its source.

Today this is the Abraham River *(Nahr Ibrahim)*, but before the Christian campaign to wipe away the old creeds from the landscape, the river was sacred to Tammuz, a minor Babylonian deity and lover of Ishtar, the mother earth goddess. Every summer he died, and Ishtar, in grief, abandoned her charge of the earth to search for him and so the ground became barren in the heat of July or Tammuz, as it is still known in Arabic. But it is by the Greek name Adonis that the god is now remembered and the river still occasionally called. As the myths migrated westwards, Ishtar also changed her name, first to Astarte and finally to Aphrodite. As the names changed, so the stories grew and diversified, taking a special root in this valley.

On the trail of a myth, we set off to Afqa, to find the source of the river and a story that would fit the scenery. Appropriately for a river steeped in legend, the source was a spectacle. There were no tiny streams or damp meadows spawning minor tributaries for the river of Adonis. Born deep under the mountain, it came crashing out of a deep cave high above the valley, a continuous avalanche of water.

Whatever the origins of the god, and there are many versions of the story, it was here that Adonis met his end. A common thread through all the tellings is that he was a beautiful youth loved by Aphrodite, leading to his inevitable downfall at the hands of jealous gods. Killed by a Wild Boar, his death gave life to the mountain meadow as scarlet anemones grew from his drops of blood, a crimson rebirth. It is said that the river runs red each spring, after the winter rains, in memory of his death, as the ochre soil leaches into the watercourses all the way down to the sea. But we were exploring the ancient temple blocks that scattered the site in the month of Tammuz, July, when the Semitic origins of the myth talk of the weeping of the goddess and the impotence of the earth caused by her grief.

These were myths in children's books, symbols of long-lost stories decaying in the stone. And then we came to the tree at the edge of the water in full blossom with strips of cloth weighing down the branches so that they touched the current. We were brought back to the modern day with a jolt. We discovered that Adonis went through one more mutation, and is still revered by some. St George is his name today.[49] With its long association of life, death, and rebirth, the site still draws its supplicants, Christian and Muslim alike, to ask a boon of the saint. The rags are strips from the clothing of sick loved ones and the trip is for *baraka*, blessing, to tip the balance in the favour of the suffering one.

Little is known of the real figure behind the stories of the saint, but he certainly made the transfer from East to West in grand style. The patron saint of England, he had his origins in the Near East. Most likely he was from Cappadocia in modern-day Turkey, a military Christian convert who refused to take part in Diocletian's persecution of Christians and so found martyrdom himself.[50] Like the stories of Adonis, the stories are many and competing. On an earlier trip to Syria, we visited the *Wadi el Nassara*, with its colossal medieval castle of Crac de Chevaliers. In this region the villages compete with claims to be his birthplace; still other stories point to Palestine for his origins. In any event, tales of his valour made their journey west with returning crusaders,[51] to be embellished and made our own, even to the point that his Middle Eastern cross became the English national flag.

The IBA programme took longer than we had first envisioned, as modern-day violence in the form of the 2006 war between Israel and Hezbollah both interrupted the fieldwork and made a number of locations inaccessible due to the huge number of cluster bombs left behind. But even with these interruptions, the conclusions were far

[49] Colin Thubron, *The Hills of Adonis*, New York, NY: Vintage, 2008, p. 125.

[50] www.bbc.co.uk/history/historic_figures/george_st.shtml (accessed 5.11.14).

[51] www.britannia.com/history/stgeorge.html (accessed 5.11.14).

beyond our expectations. When we started, there were four identified IBAs in the country. By the end of the programme with our partners SPNL and Birdlife International, we had discovered eleven more.[52] Tyre beach did not satisfy the rigorous international criteria for IBA status, although it remained an important site for Mediterranean dune plants and reptiles. However, the glorious mountain refuge of *Jabal* Moussa bounded by the Abraham River was given full IBA status.

In some ways, the easy part of the IBA project was the fieldwork that identified the areas most important for conservation. The second part, where we attempted to engage the communities living alongside or even in the sites in their protection, was trickier. Some of the new IBAs already had keen local groups, either because they were designated nature reserves or there were groups pushing for that declaration. In either case, the news that their beloved wood, valley, or wetland was to be given an international star rating for conservation was enthusiastically received, and our further involvement was welcomed with open arms. For a few sites, however, advocating for the protection of the areas was much harder work and even finding a local body that had an interest in conservation proved difficult in one or two cases.

Whether we were given the red carpet treatment or had to put in long days to develop a conservation coalition of the willing, the second phase of the programme was the same. Together with colleagues from SPNL we trained up to twenty or so reserve managers, rangers, guides, guards, teachers, or just local enthusiasts at each new IBA in bird identification and conservation, advocacy, and site protection. Many of these week-long courses in the mountains, forests, valleys, and hills of Lebanon were memorable times. Memorable as we taught eager young conservationists something of the beauty, complexity and fragility of the wildlife on their village doorsteps; memorable because I continued to learn so much of the beauty, complexity, and fragility of the people and communities surrounding these very special sites.

---

[52] www.arocha.org/lebanoniba (accessed 5.11.14).

The training course we ran furthest from Beirut, and home, was in the far northern section of Mount Lebanon, in the newly declared IBA known as "the upper mountains of Akkar-Donnieh". This was not an area I knew prior to the course, as the fieldwork had been carried out by our friends at SPNL. They had discovered a rich birdlife with good populations of important regional specialities,[53] like the White-throated Robin, Pale Rock Sparrow and Crimson-winged Finch as well as a tremendous diversity of flowering plants in rich habitats of Turkey Oak, fir, Cedar of Lebanon, and juniper.

The start of this large site of over 5,000 hectares had the intriguing name of *Wadi Jouhannam*, the valley of hell, and it was here that we decided to take the university students, local councillors, and high school teachers that made up the course participants. My job was to teach the bird identification modules, giving the students the framework and tools that would enable them to hone their own birdwatching skills so that they could act as guides and teachers of others. In this region on the margins, deep economic problems came with the wild beauty and unspoilt vistas. It was a niche for eco-tourism that was being trialled by an innovative social enterprise NGO. It was great to know that the skills developed could help bring employment opportunities, but an even greater thrill to see the natural world opening up to these curious young people as they discovered the secret stories of the birds flying overhead.

We had set up the classroom in the main hall of the village mosque; the local sheikh was a gracious host. He had formally opened the proceedings and sat through many of the talks, clearly enjoying adding to his own knowledge of the natural world. He came up to me at the coffee break, after I had been teaching about how birds are adapted to their habitats and feeding strategies, using beak shape and size to match feeding strategy, from the fishing harpoons of herons to the fine probing bills of waders ideal for extracting worms and the like from mud.

---

[53] Both regionally endemic species and biome-restricted species (Irano-Turanian).

176

"In one sense, birds are Muslims, you know."

"How is that?" I asked, sipping my scalding coffee from its tiny cup.

"They live in the way Allah created for them. They obey his laws, the natural laws, the laws he created to govern them. Of course, they don't have free will like we do, but they follow their instincts and by doing that they submit to God."

And then my black-robed friend recited from the Qur'an, sura 24:41:

> *Do you not see how all that is in the heavens and earth glorifies God,*
> *And the birds with wings outspread?*
> *Each has learnt his prayer and his glorification. And God knows full*
> *well what they do.*[54]

I talked with the sheikh on and off over the next couple of days, as I did with almost all of the students. Conversation was easy; everyone was enjoying the course and developing friendships. Well, almost everyone. There were two young men, Mussa and Mohammed, who always seemed to avoid me. They were not rude, but they would never answer my questions in open class, and no matter how hard I tried, I could not corner either of them during the breaks to start a chat.

It was the afternoon of the fieldtrip to the wadi and I decided this was my chance to ask them what the problem was, as in the session before lunch I had put my finger on one of the reasons they made me so uncomfortable. There were a handful of shy participants who I had hardly spoken to, but what was different about these two lads was that they assiduously refused to look me in the eye. They tried not to draw attention to it, but as I became more aware, it became more and more obvious to the point that I felt offended. I would have asked the sheikh if I had upset them

---

[54] Khaldi, *The Qur'an: A New Translation*, p. 285.

in some way, but he had gone into town for meetings. So I asked the high school teacher who the younger students referred to as Madame Rima for words of advice before I confronted them.

Having explained my observations, she laughed uproariously and then drew me to one side away from the group so no one could hear. I must confess this was not the reception I had expected, and it had not improved my mood.

"They are worried you have the evil eye," she said, boldly.

"But that is ridiculous – why do they think I mean them harm?"

"Think of it from their perspective. You don't see many people with blue eyes here – they may not have actually met anyone with eyes like yours, and they are afraid of the evil eye. It is nothing personal."

Whereas St George was a source of blessing, the evil eye meant malice and harm. Many of our friends and neighbours dismissed it as superstition, but for Mussa and Mohammed and many others, the power of the evil eye was very real. Originating in envy, precious people or things were particularly vulnerable to a look from someone with jealousy in their heart. For those who lived in fear, it was an almost tangible force. Some people were thought to be best avoided as their looks were literally dangerous. Blessings were communicated through touch, but envy came in a look. The commonest protective talismans reflected the origin of the attack as they were painted or glass-eye ornaments and they were always blue.

"By the way," said Madame Rima, "Mohammed and Mussa won't come to the fieldtrip this afternoon."

"How do you know? They haven't said anything."

"The wadi is a wild place, far away from the village, and very deep. They will be worried about Jinn."

Whereas belief in the evil eye, although common, could be described as a folk superstition, Jinn formed part of the Islamic cosmology.

The Qur'an states that they were created before man from fire, but like man they have free will. They can be in submission to God as Muslims but, due to their fiery nature, many are not and form the ranks of devils under the leadership of Satan. The name "Jinn" comes from the Arabic word to conceal and they are usually invisible to human eyes. However, they can take physical form which might be human, animal, or even a tree. We heard many stories of how they use these powers for mischief and worse, oppressing the unwary and unprotected. The greatest fear is of possession, as it is believed that they can take over minds and bodies, as well as being the agents of black magic.

With this understanding of the universe, it is little wonder that Mohammed and Mussa chose to avoid the wadi.

Minus the two boys, we set off on the fieldtrip, taking a minibus halfway into the valley and then walking the last mile or so down steep winding paths. As we descended, the sides of the wadi closed in, the rock walls towering above us as we trekked deeper into the defile. Despite the warmth of the day, the path was in almost permanent shade, slippery in places with dripping moss. A hush descended on the group, the only sound the trickle of water on its way to join the river intent on grinding its way deeper into the earth. It was an oppressive silence, heavy on the back of the neck. Footsteps were muted as our earlier cacophony dribbled away in this tunnel of stone.

Suddenly there was a scream from the front of the group as a huge shadow passed over the line, strung out in single file, hemmed in by the gorge. It ricocheted around the ravine setting off small rock falls, pebbles and earth skittering in tiny avalanches, dusting our heads.

"Look up!" I shouted to those confused as to the source of the commotion. "It's an Eagle Owl."

A ripple of relief spread through the group, and friends happily recounted whether they saw the magnificent bird or just felt the rush of air over the heads. It was as if the bird had broken a spell and, with the laughter of the party, we broke out into a wider sun-soaked opening. A babbling stream took up the merriment, flowing fast over its bed of rounded boulders, a Dipper living up to its name momentarily freezing in mid-bob before it took flight. Its piping call was full of summer from the world above.

CHAPTER 12

Valentine's Day

14 February 2005
Ras Baalbek, Beirut, Lebanon

The watery sun struggled through an early morning bank of cloud on the horizon, casting weak shadows on the grit and sand of the dun-coloured landscape. Thorn bushes, more grey than green, brought scant colour to the hillsides that rose up into towering cliffs skirted by wide aprons of scree. Colin, Richard, and I had been walking since just before dawn, an early start to avoid the heat of the day and to record the birds of the desert (which, like birds everywhere, are most active early in the morning). Suddenly the sun lifted above the clouds and the hills burst into colour, as if glowing from within, deep orange and red. The level plain below us looked Martian: lifeless red sand strewn with angular pebbles and boulders now casting long shadows towards the first folds of the mountains on the other side of the valley. Our winding path, a white etching scratched along the contour of the hillside, took us to a wadi, peppered green with tufts of spiky grass.

It doesn't sound a likely contender for an Important Bird Area, but what deserts lack in numbers of species, they can make up for in the uniqueness of the plants and animals that call them home, and the northern Lebanese deserts had some extraordinary inhabitants. We'd already had a good morning, with sightings of the graceful Cream Coloured Courser, a member of the wading bird family perfectly adapted for a life far from water, together with its more robust but equally noteworthy cousin the Stone Curlew. As we followed the curve of the hill, we came to a small encampment tucked into a fold in the wall of the wadi ahead of us. Cleverly placed oil drums, rocks, and plastic sheeting completed an enclosure that used the naturally steep slope of the miniature valley for its back wall. It was brimming with black goats.

As we watched, a tracksuited teenage girl, head covering tightly wrapped around her face, was struggling with the packing case gate. Suddenly it shifted and a surge of shaggy black bodies tumbled down the short incline to the grazing on the floor of the wadi below. She encouraged the last few kids to join the flock with a few well-aimed stones, clattering behind their back hooves as they danced out of the stockade. She then made her way to the squat stone house, one of a pair, disappearing through the open door into the darkness within.

It wasn't long before a stocky, bearded man emerged from the house. He had clearly been sleeping, wrapping his red-and-white checked *kaffieh* round his head as he walked towards us.

"*Salaam alaykum*," he greeted us.

"*Alaykum asalam*," we replied.

"*Tfadilu* [Come in], join us for breakfast."

We did just that. Colin and Rich had come from the UK to join in the efforts to protect the wetland of Aammiq, and to help find other ornithological wonders worth protecting throughout the country. Ras Baalbek was at the far end of the valley and had a very different climate to the West Bekaa where the A Rocha project was based. In the rain shadow of Mount Sanine and Qornet es Sauda, it was Lebanon's driest area, but still birds and people made it their home.

The family we had met was part of an ancient tradition. Semi-nomadic goat and sheep herders, they didn't so much wander with their herds as travel between their homes. In the winter and into spring, their animals would find grazing on the scant grasses in the deserts of northern Lebanon. As the heat built and the green became a shimmering memory, they walked the flocks up into the high pastures of the mountains where they could grow fat on the alpine sward fed by the melting snows from the peaks.

We breakfasted with the family many times in the coming year as we continued the programme of fieldwork through the seasons. It was always the same delicious food: foaming warm and fresh goats' milk, a dry and pungent sheep's cheese with flatbread and sweet black tea. For half of the year this was shared in their tiny stone cabin in the barren beauty of the northern Bekaa and for six months in a low-slung tent below the shrinking snowfields of Mount Lebanon.

I was on my way home. Lost in thought, I was driving the familiar route from the Bekaa to Beirut, over the Dahar el Bayda crossing with its military checkpoint where the soldiers made each car slow for a cursory inspection. Today they were bored and just peered at the back seats, and waved me on. As I slowed to join the heavy traffic on the lower stretches of the road, the panoramic vistas of the Barouk ridge and Chouf hills well behind me, I was thinking about the two deserts I had been in that week. Images of snowy peaks looming over dusty goat herds in the north Bekaa from the last couple of days' fieldwork contrasted with the neon-lit chrome and glass bubble that was Dubai. Despite it only being February, Valentine's day, I knew the heat would be building in the emirate as last week I had swum in the warm waters of the Arabian Gulf and sat in air-conditioned offices as I wrote up the biodiversity survey I had completed as a commercial piece of work for a major contractor. As I marvelled at the different world of the Gulf Emirates, the phone rang.

I pulled into a garage forecourt to answer.

It was Susanna: "There has been a bomb, I'm…"

The line went dead.

I phoned her straight back, but there was no signal. I kept hitting redial as my mind went into overdrive.

Susanna's phone line wasn't busy, the network was down. That could only mean one thing – the authorities had shut down the mobile system to prevent any further remote detonations. The bomb must have been bad. I rejoined the highway. I needed to get to Susanna to see if she was all right.

It wasn't just my driving that was erratic. Clearly other drivers had heard news from phone calls or the radio and we were now all speeding to Beirut to find out if loved ones were OK.

It was a busy time of day to be on the main highway, but traffic gridlocked much earlier than usual, ahead of the main intersection marking entry to Beirut. While waiting three cars abreast, I wound down the window to ask a fellow driver if he knew what had happened.

"A bomb, that is all I know. But it's bad! They have shut down the Corniche, Hamra, Qoraitem and Clemenceau."

We lived in Clemenceau. It must have been close to home. Where would Susanna have been when it went off? Was it by the school? Were the kids OK? How was I going to get back if the neighbourhood was in lockdown? As we waited, conversation flowed between vehicles, drivers and passengers alike sharing titbits of information, passing on anxiety.

Eventually the traffic started moving again, the police waving us through, gesticulating with their short traffic batons. I took every backstreet shortcut I knew to avoid the mounting traffic chaos, but by the time I got to the outskirts of Hamra, it was clear I was not going to get any closer to home. Rather than join the jam, I pulled down a side street and found a car park with a space.

I ran past the attendant, dropping my lira notes into his lap as he sat transfixed, listening to the news on the radio, barely noticing me. After a few twists and turns I was on the main street that would take me through the shopping district, past the large hospital and home. But as I approached AUH (the American University Hospital) I joined the back of a huge crowd mourning as one, the women sobbing uncontrollably, the men beating their chests in grief.

"Maat, maat! He is dead, he is dead!"

Suddenly I knew who had been killed, who the bomb had been aimed at, identified by the election posters held aloft by the grief-stricken. It was ex-prime minister and leader of the largest Lebanese Sunni Muslim political party, Rafik el Hariri.

The phone rang. Thank God, it was Susanna.

"Are you all right?" I shouted into the phone, trying to make myself heard above the screaming of the crowd.

"Yes, I am home now. I am OK. I saw it. I was there. Just outside the Phoenicia.[55] They have killed Hariri!"

"I know. I am outside AUH, his body must be inside. The crowds are surrounding the hospital. I will be home in ten minutes."

When I got home, Susanna told me her story.

"I was on my way home from the travel agent and had to wait at the lights by the post office. I was at the head of the queue of cars, but when the light changed I still had to wait as the Hariri convoy shot past. You know, the usual thing: police outriders, big black jeeps, blacked-out windows, sirens blaring, lights flashing, lesser mortals having to wait." Susanna took a sip of tea to steady her nerves.

"Anyway, once they had gone through, I slipped in behind them and drove down towards the Phoenicia. They were going much faster than me so I lost sight of them as they rounded the corner, before St George's. A few seconds later, just as I drew level with the hotel, there was an enormous explosion. It was the noise that hit me first. The car rocked from side to side as I brought it to a stop. I thought I was going to be blown off the Corniche and into the marina. I ducked behind the dashboard as an enormous fireball engulfed the street ahead of me.

"A car parked at the side of the road was somersaulting in a long arc away from the detonation and a fireball erupted. As I waited to see if the inferno would engulf the car, a rattling started all around me. It was pieces of metal, tarmac, and I hate to think what else raining back down to earth. And then there was silence. Actually,

---

[55] The Phoenicia Hotel.

there must have been noise – car alarms and so on, but I couldn't hear anything. It was as if the pillar of smoke rising from the crater, the burning vehicles and the incinerated road had blocked out all sound. I don't know how long I stared at it but it was the smell that brought me back – an acrid sickly sweet smell of death.

"It sounds crazy but I suddenly thought it was an earthquake and that the Israelis were dropping bombs at the same time. My immediate thought was that there would be more bombs, so I should get out of there. I did a U-turn – nothing was coming the other way, obviously – and drove home. Even before I got to the apartment, the police had cordoned off the end of the street, but I argued with the policeman and once the fleet of ambulances had cleared, I snuck past the roadblock and into our drive. As soon as I got out of the car, the shock hit me and my legs just wouldn't hold me up. Ashraf and Ameera were lovely, they sat me down and gave me water. It was Ashraf who told me it was Hariri. I tried to phone you but didn't get much out before the line went dead."

"Have you phoned the school?" I asked, suddenly remembering the children.

"Yes, they say everything is fine. The school has not been affected and they ask that we come at the end of the day to pick up the students as normal. They don't want parents turning up early as they are trying to settle the children. The explosion was pretty loud even up by the school and the pall of smoke has been hanging over the Corniche all afternoon, so the kids are pretty jumpy. But we need to go now to get there for the end of school."

And with that all we could think about was getting to the children and all five of us being together, safe.

Our normal route to school looked like a war zone. Flanked by banks and high-end commercial property, every plate-glass shop and office front had been destroyed, a million glistening shards under an avenue of jacaranda trees. There was no traffic and the few pedestrians hurried to their destinations clutching briefcases or handbags, anxiety written into their gait. Outside each office block, employees swept in silence, sentinels marking the destruction. We passed unoccupied offices and shops torn open, violated, their contents exposed. But no one entered; there was no looting, just silence, shock, and grief.

We got to the school ten minutes before the final bell. Our children were the only students left in the building. Every other parent, on hearing the news, had turned up at school to withdraw their children.

Chloe asked: "Why didn't you come?"

Never had we felt so foreign.

"The school asked the parents not to. They asked us to wait till the end of the school day. Did any children stay for the afternoon?" Susanna asked, carefully.

"Yeah, there were three of us in my class till a few minutes ago," chipped in Sam. "The kids have just been dribbling away all afternoon. They could only go when a parent or driver came for them."

"Why did they kill Hariri?" asked Josh.

Joshua, aged seven, not only knew who had been killed but that he had been prime minister and was the political leader of the Sunni Muslims. He had been talking about "what next" with his friends all afternoon in class. Like most Lebanese schoolchildren, he knew his politics and that this was going to have far-reaching consequences.

The scale of the impact of the assassination was obvious just two days later at Hariri's funeral. He had been a dominant force in politics for more than a decade, and had reputedly been one of the richest politicians in the world. It hadn't started this way for him. He was born into a poor family in the southern town of Sidon, making his fortune in Saudi Arabia, where he ran a construction company that worked for the royal family. He returned to lead the country at the end of the Lebanese civil war in 1992 and held prime ministerial office for a total of five terms. In October 2004 he resigned when the pro-Syrian government extended the term of President Lahoud.[56]

---

[56] www.bbc.co.uk/news/world-middle-east-13978635 (accessed 5.11.14).

On the day of the funeral, the crowds went past our apartment block all morning. All traffic was stopped. Beirut was at a standstill. Schools, offices, banks, businesses, everything was closed. The citizens of Beirut and wider Lebanon were either watching the funeral events unfold on TV or they were walking, on their way.

Much to the annoyance of Sam, I said he had to follow British Foreign Office advice and stay away from public demonstrations as the situation was unclear and volatile. But I had to go.

I felt a compulsion to stand alongside our friends and neighbours, to walk with them in their national journey of grief. The crowds were immense streaming downtown. The mood was sombre. Like all Middle Eastern funerals, this was just a matter of forty-eight hours (usually even less) after the bereavement, so the loss was still raw. The political rage was barely subdued, but it had been put to one side for the day, to mark the passing of the man. Tomorrow would be the time for demonstrations. The crowds were mourning the ex-prime minister and his bodyguards who had been killed, Bassel Fleihan, the ex-finance minister and uncle of one of Joshua's best school friends, the twenty-one others who had died, and the hundreds who were injured in the blast. They were also mourning a litany of names who had been assassinated by similar bombs over recent years; Muslim, Christian, and Druze.

With the thousands coming from the Sunni Muslim strongholds of West Beirut, I walked to the epicentre of grief, Martyrs' Square. The old statues, riddled with bullet holes from the civil war, looked down in their own misery at the crowds that carried photos of their newest martyr. Despite the security and the importance of many of the mourners, the funeral was a very public affair. The pallbearers struggled to navigate the crowd as they carried the coffins aloft, jostled by the human sea ebbing and flowing around them. Black limousines had whisked the politicians and family away long before I reached the grave site. The crowd was thinning but all could still pay their last respects at the newly dug graves, the fresh earth a more poignant picture of death than the shrine that was forming to the new Sunni saint.

The Cedar Revolution started with demonstrations. Foreshadowing the Arab Spring, still almost five years away, the drama was played out on the street. Exactly a week after the assassination, tens of thousands of protestors held a rally at the site of the murder and called for the withdrawal of Syrian troops, an end as they saw it to occupation, pointing the finger of guilt at Damascus. They believed Hariri's stand against Bashir al Assad's meddling in Lebanon's politics had cost him his life. There was growing boldness on the street; anti-Syrian slogans were everywhere. People spoke openly against the Assad regime, no longer the stuff of whispers to the trusted few. International pressure started to mount: President Bush repeated calls for Syria to withdraw its troops, and the European Union called for an independent international investigation into the assassination.[57]

But not everyone felt this way. On 8 March 2005, Hezbollah organized a mass rally to applaud Syria's role in the country and reject Western "interference".[58] The crowd was enormous and dwarfed the anti-Syrian protests of the preceding weeks. Using the megaphone of the street the pro- and anti-Syrian factions were trying to out-shout each other. All demonstrations were decked in the Lebanese flag and the national anthem always played.

The nation held its breath for the next rally. The ball was in the court of the anti-Syrian alliance who were now organizing their definitive show of popular support. The date was set for 14 March, the day I had to go over to the Bekaa for an important meeting with the team. I arrived early in the morning and clock-watched throughout the session. As soon as we had concluded, I excused myself and left to join the growing convoy on its way to Beirut. It was like joining a party on wheels. Every vehicle was draped in the national flag or the blue of Hariri's Future group. We took up the whole road, mostly occupying both lanes, as it seemed half of

[57] http://news.bbc.co.uk/1/hi/world/middle_east/4283543.stm (accessed 5.11.14).
[58] http://news.bbc.co.uk/1/hi/world/middle_east/4329201.stm (accessed 5.11.14).

the Bekaa was heading to Beirut. Like a great herd, we moved to a single destination, except I wasn't trying to get to the rally. I was trying to get home. Cars, busses, and trucks had to be abandoned, parked miles out from the centre of town, but the crowds just walked, streaming in on foot to the largest rally ever held in Beirut.

On 27 April 2005 the last of the Syrian troops left Lebanon. Although celebrated by many it was an uneasy victory. The bombings did not stop, and there were several high-profile assassinations of leading anti-Syrians, as well as a wave of bombs in Christian areas in the months to come. The divided populace were given new labels by these historic times. The pro-Syrian alliance that formed to rally its supporters was named the 8 March bloc, and 14 March identified the anti-Syrian political parties that brought out the larger crowd a few days later.

Alliances have shifted somewhat over the years since 2005 although the vast majority of Shia political support is to be found in 8 March whereas the Sunnis are near universally in 14 March. For the Druze and Christians it is a more complex story, with most but not all Druze supporting 14 March, and the Christians more evenly split.

We had to move apartment in 2005 as our absent landlord was returning from London to retire in his native Beirut. Ironically, the political instability that followed the Hariri assassination made this easier than it would otherwise have been. Rents were depressed and prospective tenants fewer than usual and so, despite its prime location, we were able to find an available apartment even closer to the children's school, complete with a small balcony overlooking the green campus of International College and down to the sea.

All had been arranged for the day of the move. The boxes were packed, the removal company booked and the date set with the respective landlords, old and new. And so it was a huge annoyance when, on the morning of the move, the owner of the building we were vacating, and brother of the old landlord, stopped me in the corridor as we were loading the first set of boxes into the lift.

"You can't use the lift to move your stuff," he snapped.

"Why not?" I enquired, with a calm I did not feel. "This is the sixth floor. It will take us forever to carry it all down the stairs."

"Your furniture will be too heavy and it will break the lift. You can't use the stairs either," he added. "These workmen will damage the stairwell, scrape the paint, and knock holes in the plaster."

He turned as if to go.

"How are we supposed to move our belongings if we can't use the lift or the stairs – drop them out of the window?" I ridiculed him, no longer trying to mask my annoyance.

"Hire a crane, of course," he said, disappearing down the corridor.

I went back into the apartment to find the foreman who was organizing the furniture for the next load. I explained what the building's owner had just said.

I was in full rant: "How ridiculous is that! Even if we could hire a crane we would probably need to book it weeks in advance. I am sorry. I think we will have to go down and talk to the guy together. Maybe if you reason with him, he will see how ridiculous he is being, but I think he is going to insist that we don't use the lift. Will your guys be OK carrying everything down six flights?"

"Don't worry. You can hire a crane," he said, brightly. "It will cost a bit but I can phone a friend. He will have one here in an hour."

And he did; he phoned and had a crane at the apartment block in forty minutes.

Several weary hours later, I was left at the empty flat cleaning while Susanna supervised operations at the other end, beginning the mammoth task of unpacking. As I swept the floors the phone rang, echoing around the bare walls. It was Colin, our scientific officer from the UK, living in the Bekaa.

"Hi Chris," came his strained voice. "Do you have a minute? I think I have been detained by an armed militia."

"Are you hurt? What happened and where are you?"

"I am in the eastern Bekaa. I was birding at a new site and decided to climb the hill behind that would give me a good overview of this wetland area that I have wanted to explore for a while. It seems that the hill is a military camp, not the Lebanese army, though. I think it is a Palestinian group. Anyway, I was quickly surrounded by these guys in military fatigues and with some serious guns and escorted to a hut, where I am now. They brought in the commander. I have tried to say I was just birdwatching, but my Arabic isn't great under stress and I don't think they believe me. Can you talk to them?"

"Of course. Hopefully we can do all this by phone, but if not, I will tell them I will drive up to the Bekaa and discuss it all face to face. Put them on."

And so, on this day full of surprises, I spent the next twenty minutes negotiating Colin's release from an armed unit of the Popular Front for the Liberation of Palestine. By the end I was promising to visit and show them some of the birding spots around their hill, and Colin was happily reunited with his passport, which they had previously confiscated, and back in the project jeep driving home.

What a day!

CHAPTER 13

A Summer War

2006
Menara, Beirut, Lebanon

The children responded to the political tension in very different ways. Sam followed the news, avidly charting each twist and turn. Chloe tried to ignore it and Joshua was more concerned with Cartoon Network than the news, unless school was closed because of another bomb and then, although pleased to be home, he became increasingly anxious. But by July 2006 it had been quite a while since there had been any significant trouble and we were keen to live our normal lives and get on with the things we loved doing. It was holiday time, the children were off school and in a few days cousins would be joining them from England. In planning our week before the big arrival we had tried to cater for all tastes, never an easy task with children, but we thought we had cracked it this time.

Today Sam had taken his first solo trip over the mountains, using the amazing beaten-up minibuses so common in the Middle East, Africa, and Asia that wait at major junctions to fill up and then deposit and pick up passengers anywhere along the route. He was off to birdwatch at the marsh. Susanna and Chloe were at a water park and would drop by a friend's birthday party on the way home, and Josh and I would have a father and son day, starting at our favourite café. Josh had ordered a doughnut and a shockingly blue drink with crushed ice while I stuck to a more conservative coffee and croissant for breakfast.

The café was on Bliss Street, named after one of the missionary founders of the American University of Beirut, and a popular hangout for the student set. We had just walked through the green delight of the university gardens. Set in terraces rising from the sparkling Mediterranean, the grounds climbed to the main gate, with its biblical inscription for all who pass under it: "That they may have life and have it more abundantly." The verse from John's Gospel certainly resonates through the grounds as they remain a verdant haven, breathing, alive.

I was half-listening to Josh as he was giving a graphic account of the game he had played with friends the week before. Sparing no detail, he was extolling the electronic wizardry of the console his pal Faisal had brought to class and which every boy now wanted. I was enjoying the coffee, the hubbub of animated voices, the cool breeze of the fan and Joshua's happy babble. But something was gnawing at the corner of my mind. The TV that had been no more than a background distraction had changed. The banal pop video had been replaced with an urgent screen. First there was a picture of a village in the south and then a border fence, soldiers, and tanks. Others in the café had noticed the change and conversation died, all eyes on the TV. Only Josh carried on talking.

"Just a moment, Josh. Can I watch this for a minute?" I asked.

"What is it? What has happened? Is it a bomb? Is everything OK?" asked my nine-year-old, the anxious questions tumbling out.

"No, it's not a bomb. I don't know what it is. Hold on," I replied, trying to sound calmer than I felt.

The student nearest to the TV rose to turn up the sound. Accounts were garbled but news was coming in from the south that there had been a major cross-border raid. Under cover of rockets launched into northern Israel, a group of Hezbollah fighters had attacked a patrol on the Israeli side of the fence. Three soldiers were dead, two wounded, and it appeared that two had been captured by the Lebanese militia. Four more Israelis were then killed when a tank was destroyed as it tried to retrieve the captives, and a further soldier died in the mission to bring back the bodies of the Israeli dead from inside Lebanon.

We didn't need to hear the political analysis from the television station's reporter, filmed outside the Lebanese parliament buildings, to know that Israel was going to respond and respond hard. The question was, what would they do and how quickly?

I tried to phone Susanna, without success. Sam didn't have a mobile phone.

"Great!" I thought. "My fifteen-year-old son is somewhere in the Bekaa, Susanna and Chloe are away swimming at a water park in the mountains, and a major military intervention is likely somewhere in the country today."

Almost with one motion, the crowd of young students drew out mobile phones from pockets and handbags. They were all soon deep in conversation or rapidly texting friends and family, spreading the news of the developing situation. The crowd thinned as one after another they drifted out of the café and home. Josh and I followed suit, stopping en route at the local mini-market to stock up on milk powder, flour, eggs, bread, tinned meat, and vegetables. With minor differences, all the customers in the store had the same shopping basket, as we made our practical and mental preparations for uncertainty, unsure how long the provisions would have to last and whether the shops would be open tomorrow.

The rest of the day was an anxious wait as the family regrouped. Meanwhile, the cross-border rhetoric heated up. A statement by the Lebanese Shiite group insisted on a prisoner exchange and warned against confrontation. Ehud Olmert, the Israeli prime minister, stated that the capture of the soldiers was "an act of war".[59] The uncompromising words quickly turned to violence as Israeli planes struck Hezbollah positions and roads and bridges in the south of the country.

---

[59] http://news.bbc.co.uk/1/hi/world/middle_east/5179434.stm (accessed 6.11.14).

In the balmy warmth of the late afternoon, Beirut was silent. We looked over the tops of the cypress trees and through the green grounds of International College to Mount Lebanon, distant and hazy above the millpond-still Mediterranean. As we sat watching the landscape drift into sleep, the first twinkling lights appeared on the hillsides across the bay. We felt a huge sense of relief that we had all the family under the one roof, and knew that countless families up and down the country would be feeling the same. But Beirut is only ever silent when something is wrong; the city was holding its breath. The streets were empty. There were no car horns, no traffic, or cries from children playing, no music from neighbourhood apartments, or street vendors hawking their wares. Silence… but not peace. An anxious brooding weight like summer dust settled over the country as countless families gathered, ate, prayed, and waited for whatever the night would bring.

We woke the next morning to the distant rumble of bombing. From our long years in the Bekaa we had become very familiar with the rolling growl of bombs exploding at a distance. We learned from the news that the airport had been hit and was now closed, the beginning of an Israeli blockade. We followed the news, we listened to analysis, we phoned friends and talked to neighbours. Normal life was put on hold as we waited to see how the conflict developed. Would it last a few days, as had often been the case, or were we in for the long haul? Would the international community bring pressure to bear on the two sides for a quick resolution, or would commanders press the conflict to strategic ends?

Without any answers it was hard to break the cycle of "What will we do if…?" that dominated conversation; the "we" in the extended dialogue including international and local team members and a young British volunteer in the Bekaa, as well as the family in Beirut. Once the airport was bombed there was one question that had a simple answer: we weren't going to be visited by British family members this summer. Even though we didn't have many answers it was clear that we needed to make plans; plans that were contingent on a range of possible scenarios. Drip fed by constant news and with very little else to do, it was easy to get tied up in knots over possibilities. Anxious phone calls from the UK and the stifling heat added to a growing sense of restless apprehension.

It wasn't long before we were getting some of the news first-hand – watching fighter jets over the city, hearing the bombing and seeing the destruction. It had only been on Wednesday morning that I was in the café with Josh: by Friday of the same week there were massive air strikes all over Lebanon and scores of *Katyusha* rockets were being fired into northern Israel.

The nights were particularly long and difficult. There would be hours of bombing, mostly over the Shiite-dominated southern suburbs, a stronghold for Hezbollah. The near-constant rumble was occasionally punctuated by a massive detonation close by, perhaps at the Beirut port or a key bridge in the city. Miraculously, the children slept through it all, but Susanna and I lay awake, tossing and turning, the heat building, the fans idle without electricity as it was now in shorter supply than ever following the bombing of the power station just down the coast.

After a little sleep we would turn on the TV, if the electricity allowed, to see the consequences of the bombing that had seemed ethereal and dreamlike in the early hours. The scenes were cataclysmic: whole districts with their apartment blocks shattered, spewing rubble into great mounds, the streets smothered. Incinerated cars lay on pockmarked roads and bridges were ripped apart, huge craters like gaping maws marking the once central divide. Everywhere there was shattered concrete with pancaked buildings and always the dead, carried in grief, or in blue body bags laid out in orderly rows.

If we tuned into the BBC we would also see the damage inflicted on northern Israel by the indiscriminately launched rockets, which produced a more singular suffering: a car destroyed, a family distraught, an apartment block damaged. But on both sides the conflict sent populations on the move and the world watched while refugees poured out of range of the random rockets or away from the next military target.

For us, a first threshold had been reached with the bombing of roads and bridges outside the south. We needed to relocate the foreign team members to Beirut while they could still cross the mountains. The escalating crisis meant that an evacuation had to be a possibility, and if that was to happen, it would be from Beirut. Our local colleague Ramzy lived in Zahle, which he felt was as safe as anywhere could be in Lebanon that summer. The nearly 100 per cent Christian town, secure in its mountain valley, was not a target for the Israeli war planes. Mary Kopti, our church worker, lived just around the corner from us, and so with her husband was a major source of local knowledge, wisdom and advice in a fast-changing situation.

We were more on edge than usual as we waited for Colin, Rich, Veronique, and Isabelle to get to Beirut. We jumped with every explosion, each time telling ourselves that the detonations weren't coming from the direction of the Damascus highway upon which our friends were travelling. When they finally reached us, they said their journey had been a white-knuckle ride as they passed through destroyed villages, military aircraft crossing the skies above them. Isabelle, a young A Rocha volunteer who had come to do a landscape architecture internship, moved in with us, while the other three stayed at the All Saints' vicarage, an apartment in a block about half a mile away from us, as Nabil, the vicar, and family were away on holiday.

With the situation escalating, the days were never-ending and the nights interminable. We had stocked ours and the team's cupboards with non-perishable foods, by quick forays to the half-open mini-markets of Hamra. We kept in touch with friends and family and followed updates of British Foreign Office advice. We watched the news and listened to the radio. We played endless games of Monopoly and cards and talked and prayed. Just three days in and we were going stir-crazy.

I needed to get out and Sam and Chloe were as keen as me to walk along the Corniche and to smell the sea, just a few hundred yards from our apartment. There hadn't been any bombing close by that morning, and we had worked out that as long as we stayed away from any strategic or quasi-military installations, we should be fine. It was truly fantastic to get out of the apartment. We were not alone as a few others jogged or walked by the sea and there were even a few cars on the street, hurrying to their destinations. We crossed over the carriageway to walk on the seaside pavement, past the lighthouse and towards the iconic Uncle Deeks, the coffee shop that serves Beirut's army of delivery men, their motorized scooters usually in serried ranks alongside its bright blue awnings advertising American cigarettes.

We hadn't gone far when a colossal explosion rocked the ground. Laughing Doves dropped from the sky as the percussion wave hit them. Automatically we turned to see the lighthouse engulfed in flame. We had been right in our assessment as to the type of places to avoid, but not broad enough in our analysis of what might count as a strategic installation.

Despite the closeness of that missile strike, by the next Sunday we all needed to get out of the flat. It wasn't just being housebound: we needed to feel we could make some choices, that we could decide to carry on with something from our normal lives, and that the agenda was not all set by war. We phoned around. Others felt the same, and so we decided to run a small church service at the vicarage. It wasn't far. We would take the car and park in front of the apartment block. The others were either already there or lived close by.

The drive was tortuous and tense. On several occasions bright flashes lit the sky like lightning with its consequent thunder. The service was extraordinary. It wasn't easy singing the hymns above the rattling windows and intruding explosions but the prayers were fervent and the fellowship deep.

On our return, we realized that although it was vital to feel that we weren't prisoners in our own home, it was also important to acknowledge that home meant safety, particularly for the children. Although statistically we were very unlikely to be harmed as long as we stayed indoors, the emotional and psychological health of the family was at serious risk the longer the situation continued. As the conflict deepened and the rhetoric became ever more bellicose, we realized we had big decisions to make about the potential evacuation now openly talked about by the Western powers, including Britain. We were glad not to be alone in the decision-making. We took advice from the A Rocha Lebanon board and the British Embassy, from friends and neighbours, and above all, our employers, Interserve. In the end we were given a mandatory evacuation order.

These decisions are never simple and it is easy with hindsight to say we would have been OK to stay, but international agencies have multiple issues to address. They need to assess the risk of physical and emotional harm from staying, and balance that with the threat to safety of fleeing. They need to consider whether their staff can achieve anything in the country or are a potential liability to local churches and partner organizations. They need to predict the likely duration of the conflict and assess long-term trauma from a prolonged state of stress.

In any event, the decision had been taken and we knew it was necessary. We also recognized that my staying would greatly increase the trauma for the family, and so we decided that we would all leave together. The way out was clear as two ships, HMS *Gloucester* and *York* were steaming towards Beirut, evacuation offered to all British citizens who wanted it. The question that remained was: when?

This question was uppermost in the minds of the British media as headlines criticized the tardy pace of the evacuation effort. With typical national interest, the matter of the British evacuees was high up the nightly news bulletins and Britain unfavourably compared to the one or two nations that had already got its citizens out to safety. We were sitting playing yet another game of blackjack when the telephone rang, bringing the British media's interest in the story home to us in a way we least expected.

"Hi Chris, Karen here," said the familiar voice on the other end of the phone.

"Hello Karen, you OK?" I replied. "How are things in Tripoli? Are you and Mike all right?"

"Yes, we're fine. We're not in Tripoli, though. Because Mike works for the British Council, we've been drafted in to help with the logistics of the evacuation planning. I assume you are going?"

"Yes, we have been told to by our employers, but in any event, it's right for the kids. It seems awful, though, doesn't it? We can leave. Our kids can get out, but the Lebanese kids can't. We want to avoid trauma, but what about our neighbours and friends?"

"I know what you mean, but all our neighbours just tell us to go as soon as we can. They don't hold it against us that we have a way out and they don't. It's humbling. But that is not why I phoned."

"Go on."

"We have a journalist here who wants to follow the story of a British family as they get evacuated."

"Sounds awful. Which paper is he from and why us?"

"He is not from a paper; he is from ITN – the television news – and they want a family that look British."

"What do you mean – don't other Brits look British?"

"The media is all over this story and the numbers bandied about are up to 22,000 British and dual nationals in the country. They reckon around 5,000 want to be evacuated. The vast majority of those are dual citizens or the business community without kids. You guys will look the part."

"That's crazy. I don't want to be difficult but it is stressful enough to be stuck in the apartment all day with all that is going on. I really don't want to add a journalist into the mix."

"No worries. I said I would ask. Keep safe and see you on the ship."

I rejoined the family card game.

"Who was that?" asked Susanna.

I explained the request. When I had finished relating the gist of the call I was greeted with a storm of, "You said what?"

"Seriously," Isabelle spoke for the group. "Sounds fun, it's not as if we're busy. And if we are on TV we are bound to get an early slot in the evacuation."

So I phoned Karen back and Andrew from ITN appeared at the front door a few hours later.

For a few nights we appeared regularly on the British television news – a human interest story to give a face to some of the trauma of a conflict engulfing a nation. In many ways it seemed trivial and false. We were very much at the fortunate end of the spectrum. Our immediate neighbourhood was not targeted for attack and we had an escape route only open to a lucky few. ITN reported faithfully on the wider conflict but long minutes of prime-time news was spent on the British government's plans for evacuation. The angle our new journalist friend clearly wanted was to present a war-traumatized family desperate to leave and critical of the delay. In truth we knew we had to go but we didn't want to and the evacuation was set in motion very quickly.

We continued holed up in the apartment waiting for the phone call to say that it was our turn to get to the port and the waiting British navy. We each had a single small backpack ready, containing the only possessions we were going to be able to take with us. And so we waited, following the progress of the war:

- Day 7: So far in the conflict, 230 Lebanese and twenty-five Israelis have been killed.

- Day 8: More than sixty Lebanese civilians are killed in raids up and down the country. Israeli troops enter southern Lebanon. There are fierce clashes with Hezbollah. Two Israeli soldiers are killed.

- Day 9: Eighty Israeli air strikes hit the country. Thirty *Katyusha* rockets are launched into northern Israel, and the death toll reaches 306 Lebanese and thirty-one Israelis. The UN secretary general calls for a ceasefire.

- Day 10: Israel masses tanks on the border. Israel hits more than forty targets, mostly in Beirut. An unexploded leaflet bomb falls in the International College campus next door to our apartment, leaving a large crater in the lawn.

- Day 11: To date, the death toll stands at 350 Lebanese and thirty-four Israelis.

- Day 12: A volley of *Katyusha* rockets hit Haifa, killing two Israeli citizens and injuring fifteen. Air raids target Beirut, the Bekaa, Tyre and Sidon with unknown casualties.

- Day 13: In southern Lebanon, there is fierce fighting around Bint Jbeil. An Israeli helicopter crashes in northern Israel, two pilots are killed. Air strikes continue on both sides of the border.[60]

We got the phone call.

We didn't get much sleep on night thirteen. It wasn't the familiar sounds of war – the heavy rumble of distant bombing or the earth-shaking roar of a closer explosion – it was the question that constantly went through our minds: would we be back?

We had organized two taxis to collect us, Rich, Veronique, Colin, and Isabelle first thing in the morning. Andrew filmed us as we locked up the apartment and said goodbye to our life in Beirut. Both taxi drivers nervously smoked cigarettes as we piled into the cars. There were tense, taut lines across their faces showing the stress of their trade, ferrying passengers through a war-torn city. Rumours were rife that cars on the road could be targets, which explained their stomach-churning manoeuvres as we hurtled towards the port. We disembarked at the mustering point to see a fireball rise, followed by the inevitable concussive boom a few blocks to the east. We later learned that an Israeli jet had mistaken a drilling rig on the back of a truck for a rocket launcher.

---

[60] http://news.bbc.co.uk/1/hi/world/middle_east/5259576.stm (accessed 6.11.14).

From a war zone, we entered a world of queuing, processing, and waiting – lots and lots of waiting. Once the officials were certain of our paperwork and HMS *York* was prepared, we boarded the ship. With the other families, we were taken deep below decks where we found narrow benches squashed among the military hardware to sit out the five-hour crossing to Cyprus. Once in Limassol, the processing continued. From the time we got into the taxis to our last weary queue, we had been travelling for seventeen hours. We were bone-tired and deeply depressed.

Thinking the ordeal was nearly over, we found ourselves in a blind alley in the processing line. As we watched, fellow passengers filed past us to be stamped and cleared while we had to sit, drained, with three emotionally exhausted children asking when they could sleep. My well-intentioned request to the British official that we be allowed to progress had been met with surly indifference followed by vindictive protocol that made us wait till the very last passenger was processed before we were allowed to proceed. It was the most difficult hour of the day and somehow the waste, the pain, and the unfairness of it all focused on this petty act of power. The British official in question had probably had an equally difficult day; she had had to leave her own Beirut home and life and now took the opportunity to vent some of her angst on this family that dared question her orders. She became a focus for the family's unhappiness in numerous rants over the next few days. But finally we did emerge from the military hangar to be met by family in the form of Nicholas, Susanna's Cypriot brother-in-law.

We stayed with Naomi, Susanna's sister, and her family in Cyprus for two weeks hoping that the war would end and we could go home. By early August there was still no sign of peace, and in any event a ceasefire would be no guarantee that it was secure enough to return. Reluctantly we realized our next journey would be to the UK, and any return to Beirut would be conditional on a level of security that still seemed a long way off.

The decision to leave Lebanon was tough, the evacuation a surreal dream. Back in the UK, the hard work really started. We didn't know how long we would be in England. We had no home in Britain, no address, no possessions, clothes, books, or toys for the kids. With no permanent address we could not register the children for school. We had a stark choice. Either we decided to relocate, to rent a house, put the kids in school and look for the "What next after Lebanon?" or we had to live an itinerant life, moving from house to house, until we could return home to the Middle East.

It was still the summer holidays and so we were able to house-hop till September, guests of friends and relatives while they were away. With the school term looming, we decided to home-school Chloe and Josh for a few weeks, buying us time, but we had to find a potentially more permanent solution for Sam as he was entering his GCSE years. Monkton Combe School came to the rescue with the generous offer of allowing Sam to enrol in the new term for a few weeks, the full term or until the end of his school years, depending on what happened in Lebanon and whether we returned or stayed in the UK. It was a very sombre family parting when we left Sam to board at the school and we drove to Birmingham where we were house-sitting.

From a distance we marked the diary of the ending of the war from radio and television news and emails from Lebanese friends:

- 11 August: UN Security Council is unanimous in its call for an Israeli–Hezbollah ceasefire.

- 14 August: after twenty-four hours of some of the fiercest fighting of the war, a UN-brokered ceasefire comes into effect.

- 15 August: sporadic violence continues, three Hezbollah fighters are killed.

- 16 August: 250,000 Lebanese have returned to their homes, and another 500,000 are on the move.

- 24 August: the UN launches a sixty-day plan to tackle the humanitarian crisis in Lebanon.

With the truce came the counting. These are the final accounts of the war:[61]

- The dead, military – 116 Israeli soldiers, and somewhere between 250 and 530 Hezbollah fighters with twenty-eight Lebanese soldiers killed who were not involved in the conflict.

- The dead, civilian – forty-three Israelis, 1,109 Lebanese.

- The injured (all classes) – 690 Israelis, 3,697 Lebanese.

- Displaced – 500,000 Israeli, 915,762 Lebanese.

- Damage – In Israel more than 300 buildings, in Lebanon 15,000 houses/apartments, 900 factories and other commercial buildings, thirty-two items of infrastructure including airports, water and electrical plants, twenty-five fuel stations, seventy-eight bridges, and 630 km of road.

- Ordnance – 3,699 Hezbollah rockets landed in Israel, in Lebanon 7,000 air strike targets hit.

Despite great uncertainty and caution, UN peacekeepers were deployed and the situation in southern Lebanon returned to an uneasy truce. And so it was with careful planning and the inevitable bureaucracy of an international agency that first I travelled back for an assessment visit and then Susanna, Josh, and Chloe returned home. To great family rejoicing, Sam joined us at Christmas at the end of his first and only term at an English boarding school.

It was the Sunday before Christmas and to our great joy we again took up a whole row at All Saints Church, Beirut. We were home and we were together. Nabil, our vicar, had just exhorted us to

---

[61] http://news.bbc.co.uk/1/hi/world/middle_east/5257128.stm (accessed 6.11.14).

share in Christ's peace as part of the service of Holy Communion: "The peace of the Lord be always with you." The congregation, so recently scattered, with some members still missing but with many restored, replied as if with one voice: "And also with you." Nabil continued with the line that always sent the parishioners into a festival of hand-clasping and hugs: "Let us share with one another a sign of Christ's peace."

Having hugged Susanna, Sam, Chloe, and Josh, I turned around to offer Christ's peace to those behind me, only to look into the horrified eyes of the British evacuation official who had been so vindictive to the family back in Cyprus, months before. During the split second double take, the words of the Lord's Prayer resonated in my head: "And forgive us our trespasses as we forgive those that trespass against us."

I could almost feel God breathing down the back of my neck: "Your turn."

"We have met before, I think you might remember. We didn't get off on the right foot. I am Chris, by the way. Welcome to All Saints Beirut. The peace of the Lord be with you."

"And also with you," came the reply.

That was a very special Sunday; we had a fantastic lunch complete with all our favourite foods that we had missed – *sambousik*, *moutabel*, *kibbe*, *homous*, and *tabouleh*. The infectious laughter of the kids rolled around the table as we caught up with Sam's stories from boarding school. At a very deep level I felt changed. We were home and we were grateful, although painfully aware of many family tables set with loved ones missing, never to return.

CHAPTER 14

The Final Departure

2008, Cyprus
2005–08 Menara, Beirut, Lebanon

I was sitting on a beach in Cyprus, enjoying the feel of salt crusting on my skin as I dried off in the late afternoon sun. It had been a great day. I had been hiking through the Akamas Peninsula, the western extension of the Troodos mountain range that juts into the Mediterranean, a world away from the tourist hustle of the Cypriot resort towns and the stresses of Lebanon. The crescent of golden sand was enclosed by low limestone cliffs forming the miniature bay I had discovered at the end of my day's ramble. I was alone on the beach and with my thoughts, which skipped from the bizarrely beautiful Spider Orchids, still blooming in the shade of the pine trees up the hill, to the family back in Beirut. Since we had returned to Lebanon eighteen months ago, after the Hezbollah–Israel war in late 2006, life and work had been very difficult. Lebanon faced a huge task of rebuilding: roads, bridges, and apartment blocks certainly, but also political consensus and economic confidence.

The work of A Rocha was increasingly national but getting round the country was much more difficult than before the war. Reconstruction started quickly, but with so much debris to clear, roads to repair and bridges to restore, it was many months before journeys were smooth again. Every trip over the mountains to the

Bekaa included frustrating delays as traffic wended its way around an obstacle course of rubble and through tiny local side streets, the main highway and tallest bridge in the Middle East having been humbled by Israeli bombs.

It wasn't just the infrastructure: political deadlock gripped Beirut. A city of tents had sprung up downtown, with opposition supporters camped out for months, paralysing the government. Meetings in town meant a long walk through military lines and razor wire, past tanks and personnel carriers as the Lebanese army patrolled the perimeter of the camp. Once inside the militarized campsite, there followed an interrogation at the opposition militia checkpoint before gaining entry to Beirut's central squares. Up and down the country it was impossible to get long-term commitments from the communities we were working with. Everyone was watching and waiting.

After eighteen months of trying to work with these constant pressures, like everyone else in the country I was stressed out and so, when the opportunity came to have a few days' break in Cyprus, I jumped at the chance. We were working on a new project, an extension of our environmental education work. We had developed a full schools visits programme at the wetland, but students and teachers alike complained that the only material available to follow up in the classroom taught through examples of American or European ecology. Our solution was the Wild Lebanon website.[62] I was collecting information and pictures of local wildlife to showcase Lebanon's own wild treasures, as Cyprus has a lot of wildlife in common with Lebanon, and the two are close. It is said, although I never confirmed it, that from the top of the Barouk ridge you can see Cyprus on a clear day.

Cyprus also has education centres introducing locals and tourists alike to the natural wonder of the Mediterranean island. I had booked a couple of appointments and hoped to bring some new ideas and photographs of wildlife away with me that I could use in the website. The visit was also a chance to have a break; a few

---

[62] www.wildlebanon.org (accessed 6.11.14).

days away from the stresses of Beirut and a chance to walk in the hills without bumping into hunters.

It was time to head back to the holiday house I was borrowing from sister-in-law Naomi, and relax with a glass of wine while I watched the sun set over Paphos, perhaps identifying the flowers I had photographed and writing up my notes from "Snake George" who I had met first thing that morning. I drove slowly over the rough terrain and back to the main track that served as a road in the pre-industrial landscape of Akamas. Leaving a trail of white dust billowing behind the car and setting the occasional stone careering off the cliff top I rejoined the twenty-first century, tarmac and the mobile phone network coverage included. Immediately my phone stirred to life as one, then a second and third text came in.

I parked at the top of the track, instinctively pulling off the road, although mine was the only car in sight, to read the texts. They were all from Susanna.

Text 1: "We are all fine, but there is fighting in the streets. Can you phone?"

Text 2: "It looks like the airport is closed."

Text 3: "The government tried to dismantle Hezbollah's communication network. Militias now on the street. You won't be able to get back till it's over. How is the holiday?"

I phoned immediately.

"Zanna, are you all OK? What is happening?"

"We are all OK, and we are all at home and safe, but can't really go out. It all started with a workers' strike today. The opposition took their opportunity and there has been street fighting on and off all day."

"Where is the fighting?" I asked, hoping not to hear the words "West Beirut" and "near us".

"Around us, really. Militias are trying to take over West Beirut because it is a government stronghold and home to Saad Hariri and Jumblatt."[63]

---

[63] Saad Hariri (son of the murdered ex-prime minister) and Walid Jumblatt, prominent 14 March political figures.

We decided I would drive to Nicosia and see if there was any way to get back to Beirut. After a few hours of sleep, I started my search to find a way to get into a war zone. The airport was completely closed and Lebanon's national carrier, Middle East Airlines, had suspended all flights until further notice. The Cyprus–Lebanon ferry had not operated in years and the few tourist ships had struck Beirut off their ports of destination. The only chance was to fly into Damascus and try to get back to Beirut overland from there. The daily flights were fully booked for the next several days as stranded Lebanese holidaymakers desperately tried to get back home. I put my name down on a waiting list and booked for five days hence, if nothing came up before.

It was a strange feeling to watch scenes as if from an action movie play out on Beirut's familiar streets, all the while wishing I was there. I kept up to date with every local development, as Susanna phoned or texted frequently. The most difficult phone call was one that I made to check that all was still OK when I had not had a text for a couple of hours.

"Hi, love. Everything all right?" I asked.

"Yeah, there is no fighting right now," Susanna replied, her light manner nearly but not quite masking a slight strain in her voice.

"What is it? Are all the kids with you?" My voice was staccato, rattling down the phone.

"Yes, we are fine. Like I said, there is a lull in the fighting and we are OK."

"And the kids?" I pressed.

"We have run out of Joshua's medicine. The doctor was quite insistent that he doesn't miss a dose, remember? We phoned the pharmacy but they won't deliver, which is hardly surprising, so we asked Samir whether he thought the lull would last. As well as being our new *natur* he seems to be part of one of the militias fighting for West Beirut. Anyway, he said it would last for two hours and so Sam has just popped up the road to get Josh's medicine. They promise to have it ready for him. The whole trip will only take twenty minutes and I was really hoping you wouldn't phone while he was out."

I prayed there and then. I also felt sick to the pit of my stomach. My son was doing what I should be doing – if only I hadn't been on holiday!

We continued talking, both of us keeping it as light and natural as we could, waiting for Sam to get back.

"Here he is. Sam is at the front door!" cried Susanna.

We both cried.

I managed to get an early flight just two days later. My last call to Susanna came with the news that the fighting in West Beirut was pretty much over. Hezbollah had won, leaving a caretaker militia drawn from the ranks of the Syrian Socialist Nationalist Party to guard the streets. The fighting had moved to other parts of the country, being particularly fierce in the Chouf mountains to the west, where our *natur*, Samir, had gone to join his Druze family and neighbours as they fought to defend the town of Chouweifat.

Even before boarding the plane, the returning Lebanese had identified one another and were huddled deep in conversation in small groups around the departure lounge of Nicosia's airport. A neatly dressed young man left the nearest conversation and came up to me, extending his right hand.

"Hi, I'm Eli. Excuse me, but are you trying to get back to Beirut?" he asked, in a broad Australian accent.

"Yes," I replied. "I live in Beirut and need to get back."

A young, immaculately dressed, coiffured young lady peeled off from the group and joined us.

"This is my wife, Yasmine. We were on our honeymoon and we have been trying to get back home ever since," Eli explained. "We need to get back to Beirut and so does the older gentleman over there. He thinks that if there are four of us we might be able to get a taxi to take us from Damascus airport to Beirut. Are you interested?"

"Yes, but won't it be pretty expensive? My name is Chris, by the way."

We walked over to Kareem and Eli introduced me. "Chris wants to get back to Beirut, too. That is four of us."

"I am interested but I don't understand why a Syrian taxi would take us into Lebanon when it is in the middle of a war," I said. "Even if they did, wouldn't it be expensive?"

"It won't be a Syrian taxi," Kareem explained. "Scores of Lebanese have been leaving every day from Damascus airport. They get there by taxi. There is no other way. So the Lebanese taxi drivers wait for the next flight in to take returnees back. They will charge a lot but, between the four of us, it won't be too bad. They will be going back anyway, so whatever they get is a bonus – better than an empty car."

From that conversation, Kareem, a banker who had been in Cyprus on business and was as keen as the rest of us to get back to family, took charge of our little party.

On arrival in Damascus, I was the last of our flight to clear passport control as my transit visa request caused some consternation, particularly as it wasn't clear through which border I would be leaving the country. As I hurried through the arrival gate, I looked anxiously around for Kareem and the others, conscious that I had delayed them by a good hour. I needn't have worried. Kareem strode across and introduced me to Tony, who had agreed to take us all home for $300 each. Relieved to have found a way back, but uncertain of what we would find when we got there, we set off in the ageing Mercedes, pumping Tony for information about the rapidly changing situation.

After navigating our way through the Damascus traffic, it was about an hour to the border in a straight line west from Syria's capital. As we got closer, conversation first faltered and then died as we waited to see if we would be allowed in to the eastern Bekaa and Lebanon. Even before we were in sight of the barricades and security paraphernalia of a Middle Eastern border, our doubts grew as we heard explosions from further up the road. Sure enough, we met a Syrian military checkpoint at the crest of the hill from which we could see the border a couple of miles beyond. As we pulled up, we knew what was coming, as the car before us was turning round and heading back to Damascus. The border was closed, with fierce fighting in Bar Elias and along the highway just inside Lebanon.

We had two more chances – the border at the far northern end of the Bekaa, entering Lebanon past Hermel, or the northern coastal crossing and in through Tripoli. As we drove north, Tony was on his cell phone checking with fellow taxi drivers who were ahead of us what they had found and what they were planning. By early afternoon we had been driving for four hours and the news came through that the northern Bekaa border had just closed but so far the road to Tripoli was clear. That was the good news; the bad news was that fighting had erupted in Tripoli.

Eventually we drove round the entire eastern and northern silhouette of Lebanon and arrived at the coastal border crossing. As always I was last through the formalities, but my travelling companions were sympathetic rather than critical, and it was a subdued but excited group that finally crossed into Lebanon that early May afternoon.

Tony explained his tactics as we approached Lebanon's northern city of Tripoli, where the Sunni majority live uneasily with an Alawite (and so pro-Syrian) minority: "I will drive at 100 miles an hour and we won't stop for anything."

In the car we were unsure whether to be more afraid of the mob armed with rifles, spikes, machetes and the occasional Kalashnikov that ebbed and flowed around us, or the erratic driving as we flew through the streets. Silently we prayed and remembered the stories passed down from the civil war years when cars would be stopped in circumstances like this and the occupants interrogated as to their sectarian identity. The wrong answer would lead to a bullet in the head. Inside the car we were Sunni, Maronite, Orthodox, and Protestant, all wanting to get home to the families that made our lives count, and were determined to stand up for one another if the car was stopped.

But the car wasn't stopped. After Tripoli, the journey was remarkably fast as we were one of only a handful of cars on the road. Tony was the hero of the day and delivered us each to our own homes, pausing long enough to ensure we were safely indoors before driving on to the next address.

So we were once again all safe and under the same roof. After the euphoria of my return and the catch-up from the last few days, Susanna and I turned to a conversation that had long been brewing, brought to a head by the latest violence. How long could we stay? What effect was it having on the family, the schooling of the kids? And as we looked to the next phase as Sam left school and attended a British university, did we want to run our lives in two countries with the levels of insecurity that we had lived through for years? And how had the country come to this point anyway?

Like many of our Lebanese friends and neighbours we had been buoyed by hope back in 2005 when sweeping changes followed the Cedar Revolution. The huge demonstrations on the heels of Hariri's assassination seemed to galvanize the country as it took steps to chart its own future, throwing off the yoke of the past. How could war erupt, around our own home, just three years later, as anti-government forces took up arms against neighbourhoods loyal to the country's elected representatives? The answer to that question lay back in 2005 when it was easy to get carried away with the euphoria of the demonstrators chanting "*hurriya-siyada wa istiqlal* (liberty, sovereignty, and independence)" while forgetting the divergent narratives that had brought the country to this point. It is claimed that one in every four residents of the country descended on Martyrs' Square on 14 March 2005, demanding an end to Syrian hegemony, Lebanon's largest ever public demonstration.[64] However, it must be remembered that the day was declared in reaction to the mass rally a week earlier when the same streets were filled with Lebanese thanking the Syrian regime for the fifteen years of peace that in their view Syria had helped to secure.

---

[64] A. Knudsen and M. Kerr (eds), *Lebanon: After the Cedar Revolution*, London: Hurst & Company, 2012, p. 166.

We had had the privilege of getting to know Lebanese friends from each confession who would be retelling these years from their different perspectives, but now it was time to write a different chapter for our own family. We decided the wear and tear on us all was taking its toll and that for the next family phase, with children launching into adult life, we wanted to be in the UK, helping Sam and then Chloe and Josh navigate a whole new country that just so happened to coincide with their nationality. We started to have the difficult discussions with the A Rocha Lebanon board of trustees, the Skaff family and partners up and down the country, but we had set our sights on another adventure – England.

CHAPTER 15

A New Country

2009
The Cotswolds, England

It is not true to say that living in England was new. I was born in Sussex and lived in southern England until I was thirty-two. Susanna had lived in Britain from her mid-teen years until we left for the Middle East and the children knew the country from visits back every couple of years, with two extended stays for nearly three months each. Apart from these furloughs, we had not lived in the UK as a family, except for when Sam and Chloe were babies, and we knew that this time we were back to settle, at least for a while.

To be honest, we dreaded it.

You are probably thinking, "What is wrong with this family?" and that might be fair. We had decided we needed to leave Beirut and had the extraordinary luxury of relocation with a right to live in a West European democracy with good work prospects, a free health service and world-class education. So what was the problem?

The answer is that there wasn't one problem, rather 1,000 little ones that when taken together add up to major cross-cultural stress. The fact that most people kindly assumed that we must be delighted to be back just added to the difficulty – "You must be so pleased to be home" being the commonest greeting we received in the early months after our arrival.

So what were the 1,000 little things that added up to the culture shock of re-entry for Susanna and me and the immersion experience of the "hidden immigrants", Sam, Chloe, and Josh? Let's start where every British conversation starts, with the least controversial subject of all: the weather.

"Dad, it's raining again," Josh said accusingly, mournfully staring out of the window of the cottage we were renting. We now lived in the gloriously English Cotswolds, so that we could get Chloe into Oxford to continue her studies for the International Baccalaureate and Josh to Kingham Hill, the school that felt able to pick up from his somewhat eccentric educational history.

"No, it's not," disagreed his brother. "The rain is going up! Dad, what is this crazy place doing now?"

On glancing out of the window I settled the argument: "Yes, Josh, it is raining. It's very fine rain and the wind is catching it, so it's swirling around outside the house."

"Fine rain, drizzle, showers, steady rain, pouring rain, sheets of rain, raining cats and dogs, and now uphill rain. We have had it all! Dad, is there any other sort of rain that we should know about?" asked Sam, and he stamped up the stairs, still muttering.

It was the amount of rain and lack of sunshine that first struck the family on our return to the British Isles in the summer of 2009. But as we lived through our first year, more profound differences started to affect us. As we moved into autumn and winter it was the shortening day length that had the most dramatic effect. Susanna, who was born in the tropics, and the children, who had grown up in the Eastern Mediterranean, were used to a much more equal length of day throughout the year. In the summer, the long days were an oddity, a quirky but interesting aberration. In the winter, the days that had barely started as we left the house but had finished long before we returned home were deeply unsettling. It felt as if there was something wrong with the country and it left a deep unease within the family, not helped by the trees gunmetal-cold and bare for five months of the year in a landscape bereft of colour.

If the family's thermostats and light metres were set for warmer climes, their internal navigation systems were also set to pick up different cues than were given off by the English road network. In Lebanon there were few road signs but orientation was always possible by reference to the mountains that were the backbone of the country, or the sea, running along its entire length. In England's more muted landscapes, the main roads are skilfully embedded, embankments and tree plantings masking the traffic from towns and villages and the cars from much of the surrounding geography. This is not a navigational problem for local drivers as there is an excellent road signage system. However, if you don't take any notice of road signs because you haven't grown up ever seeing one, you get lost – repeatedly. Town names didn't help much, either; they seemed so odd. When you are used to names like Majdal Tarshish, Khirbet Khanafar, Ain Kafr Zabad, and Haouch el Oumara, how do you tell the difference between Abingdon and Aberdeen or whether Salisbury is a town or the local supermarket?[65]

We had noticed, on home assignments years before, when we would tour the UK preaching in supporting churches, that the children had little idea of English geography. Having spent a few days in one suburban neighbourhood, kindly hosted by a church family, we would pack sleepy kids into the car to drive to the next housing estate destination. When the kids woke a few hours later they would ask why we hadn't left – not believing city neighbourhoods and streets could be identical hundreds of miles apart. Their impression of British uniformity was just confirmed if we took them to the town's local high street or shopping centre, as the same branded shops dominate from Dover to Dundee.

It is probably less to do with our time in the Middle East and more to do with growing up immersed in a conservation project, but the family (most of us) is allergic to shopping. I think it started soon after our arrival in the UK when we did a family shop at our

---

[65] Chloe mistook my plans for meetings in Salisbury with the normal local shopping to the Sainsbury superstore.

local supermarket. We were simply overwhelmed by the available choice. I remember looking at the butter aisle feeling paralysed – it was choice overload. In Beirut there was always plenty of butter, even two or three varieties, but shopping online at one of Britain's larger supermarket chains today and you will find more than a hundred different butter and margarine products to choose from. The consumer overabundance struck like a physical blow – and we came from Beirut, one of the Middle East's premier shopping destinations. I know of colleagues who have returned to the UK from rural Africa, Asia, and South America and collapsed in tears during their weekly grocery shop.

Now, five years in, we shop as automatically as everyone else, the choices mostly irrelevant as we hone in on the brands we like. Cross-cultural transition is a form of habituation, a normalizing to that which initially seems strange. It can resurface, however, with certain triggers, as our house often demonstrates. We are fortunate to live in a seventeenth-century converted farmhouse, made of Cotswold stone and from the timber of old ships. It is rock solid as its 350-year history attests. However, after a warm day, as it settles in for the night with mild creaks and sighs, Sam is perturbed. Before living in Oxfordshire, he had only ever lived in houses and apartments made of poured concrete and the only time they had groaned was with an earthquake or a bomb.

Although the sounds of the house bring alarm, at least there is noise. After eight years of life on a Beirut street, our village seemed rather quiet. We were amused to get a flyer through the door in the early weeks of our arrival from the nearby pub, thanking residents in advance for their tolerance of the summer outdoor music festival that would be finishing by 11 p.m. sharp on the Saturday evening. Our experience told us that street life and noise should just be picking up at this time of night. When the streets of Beirut were quiet it was never good news, and the kids still find it hard to sleep in what they experience as the crushing weight of silence outside the house.

Village life is different to city living without having to cross continents. Villagers tend to be cautious, welcoming newcomers on a "long wavelength", and when the English reserve is added in, feeling at home can take a very long time. When we first arrived, we were given the sage advice that to get to know people in the village we should get a dog. We did and we found it worked on several levels. Firstly, it necessitates getting out of the house to walk the dog and so meet people. Probably due to the infamous weather, in comparison to al fresco Lebanese social life, British socialising is a very indoor affair. A dog gets you out whatever the weather. But dog-walking works at a deeper level too. If you have a dog and you meet neighbours in the street they stop and talk to you (they talk to the dog, actually, but it is a start). This is in stark contrast to the Middle East where pet ownership is only really common in the urban Christian communities and dogs would never be seen as a social unifier.

In the British village, dogs are social harmonizers as long as certain strict rules are followed. By far the strictest of these is instant removal of any dog waste produced in a public place. Probably the worst sin possible that can be perpetrated in England's leafy lanes is leaving the offending offering on the grass verge. I am all in favour of the dramatic change in British streets since the bad old days of the 1970s when it wasn't possible to walk home from school without frequently checking the soles of one's shoes, but to this family from Beirut, the British obsession with dog mess is bizarre. The low point came when the local mayor attended our church and gave a short speech. All was well until he stated, in categoric terms, that the council was determined to deal with the worst social problem facing the town – dog poo.

Clearly different communities have different priorities and what is seen as acceptable varies too. In Beirut no one would even notice if you threw a sweet wrapper on the ground, an empty Coke can in the gutter, or a cigarette stub out of a car window. Not so in England. On the other hand, if the sun comes out in the UK for more than a few hours and the temperature rises to a comfortable 20 degrees C in the summer, there follows a mass stripping to the waist by cohorts of teenage boys and young men. This would not be a problem on a Lebanese beach, but along the local high street…?

Issues of modesty are particularly sensitive and it needs to be said that there are great swathes of middle-class England where going shirtless is as unacceptable, as it is in Beirut. But that brings us to another British baffler that the family struggle with: social class. For readers such as Sam, Chloe, and Josh who have not experienced the intricacies of the British class system, I can do no better than point you to Kate Fox's excellent book *Watching the English*, where she dissects the eccentricities of our island race with great skill and humour. An excerpt will demonstrate what outsiders and immigrants are up against:

> *A school teacher and an estate agent would both technically be "middle class". They might even both live in a terraced house, drive a Volvo, drink in the same pub and earn roughly the same annual income. But we judge social class in much more subtle ways, precisely how you arrange, furnish and decorate your terraced house; not just the make of car you drive, but whether you wash it yourself on Sundays, take it to a car wash or rely on the English climate to sluice off the worst of the dirt for you.*[66]

With topics such as class we are getting to the heart of identity, and the sensitivity stakes are rising. Another area where we need to walk lightly, but which is important in understanding cross-cultural living in the UK, is the realm of family life – and in particular, parenting. How we bring up children is greatly affected by the norms we live with, and so it is not surprising that the Lebanese and British models are so divergent. Lebanon is highly conservative in comparison to the UK when it comes to family life. Britain has had a revolution in family design, with many shapes and sizes adding to the traditional model. But whether British children are brought up

---

[66] Fox, *Watching the English*, p. 15.

by a lone parent or Mum and Dad, the family narrative in Britain is often quite different to the norms that were the setting for our family's growing years. Seen as a blessing from God, children in Lebanon join the family story. They are immediately embraced and integrated into an extended network and have a place set for them by those relationships. In England it often seems that parents reinvent themselves when children come along, and the centre of gravity and attention of the family shifts to the children.

Perhaps one simple example will illustrate the difference. For many British families, particularly during the early years, making sure the children have their meals and bedtimes consistently on time is a huge stress. Mums and dads will go to great lengths arranging their social agendas, packing food to take with them, giving strict instructions to carers, all to ensure that the children's routine is not disturbed.

We rarely saw this in Lebanon. The children came along with the family in whatever it was doing. If they were hungry they were fed, if they were sleepy they fell asleep, and it seemed that this rather more cavalier approach to infant timetabling brought up very flexible children.

Flexibility has been hugely important in our family transition of crossing cultures, as differences appear even in areas where we had naively assumed things would be the same. Language is a good example. Not Arabic, of course; we realized that we would struggle to practise Arabic in our rural county, but we didn't think we would have problems with English. At this point I must clarify that the children are fluent in their mother tongue, but as it transpires, not necessarily fluent in how it is spoken within these shores. There are two problems. The first is regional accents. Many Brits struggle with thick dialects that they are less familiar with: Glaswegian Scots has an awesome reputation for being hard to follow but Sam, Chloe, and Josh didn't know regional accents existed at all prior to relocation. They had learned all of their British English from Susanna and me, and were educated in Beirut in a mildly American international

English accent. On trips to York, Birmingham, Scotland, and Cornwall, they were convinced that they had discovered yet more languages to add to the British list, along with Gaelic and Welsh. Slowly, with exposure, these regional variations declared themselves to be English after all, and the family is now mostly able to recognize the language of home in all its regional complexity.

The second language issue, however, has been harder to untangle. Because they learned their English in isolation from a population of native speakers, they have largely missed out on the more informal, colloquial vocabulary. In the early days of settling and engagement with English, it was their early exploratory use of idioms that led to real hilarity. This illustrates what a number of our international friends have said about English: "It is an easy language to learn, but a very hard language to master." A few examples from our early days (with two-way translation for non-British readers) might help to show you how easy it is to get idioms mixed up, and so how you can end up saying something quite different to what was intended:

"We need to keep this under wrapping paper," said Josh. He was not involved in Christmas preparation, and what he should have said was: "We need to keep this under wraps", which means we need to keep it secret.

"He's a smelly egg," said Chloe. In fact, she was not referring to personal hygiene but had strayed from the actual idiom "he's a bad egg" by which she meant to say "he is an untrustworthy person".

"She's on the wagon," said Sam, confidently. He had hit on a real idiom that means "she has given up alcohol". However, what he meant to imply was that she had decided to join in now because it is fashionable, so the appropriate idiom would have been "she jumped on the bandwagon".

And finally, what would have been good advice if it wasn't for the befuddling intricacies of idiomatic English: "Don't throw the baby out of the pram." This is actually a mix-up of two idioms: "Don't throw the baby out with the bath water", which means not to lose the essential when getting rid of a small problem, and "Don't throw your toys out of the pram", which indicates a temper tantrum over something quite minor. I am not totally sure which of the two was being referenced as hilarity closed down that particular family conversation.

So, English was harder than we thought – and so was driving in England. I had assumed that the much safer English roads would be a dream in contrast to the rally-style racetrack which epitomized Lebanese driving. The reality was more complex. It is undoubtedly true that driving in Lebanon is not for the fainthearted. The combination of switchback mountain roads, largely without safety barriers, and poorly maintained lorries and trucks hauling enormous and often poorly secured loads, didn't help. But mostly it was the very different driving culture that I was looking forward to exchanging. Much like Britain, Lebanon has a tightly defined set of rules of the road: speed limits, bans on driving while talking on a mobile phone, strict driving tests, etc. However, many of them are seen more as advisory than compulsory and driving tends to be more of a white-knuckle ride than in the UK.

To my great surprise, I found that once I was back behind the wheel in England, I missed Lebanese driving and found the tightly defined traffic rules unnerving. In the UK, not only does everyone expect you to obey all the rules all of the time, but they get very upset when you make a mistake. Ending up in the wrong lane on unknown roads, waiting too long when the lights have changed or the unforgiveable sin of stalling the car can invoke a tirade of road rage out of all proportion to the misdemeanour. It is not only at the level of fellow drivers, either; if you do happen to go a little too fast you are quite likely to be photographed and fined for the privilege. In my early months of driving in the UK, I longed for the more flexible and forgiving Levantine attitude.

And what about us now, after five years in the UK? How English is the family? On a scale of one to ten, where would we rate ourselves? My answer would be on a spectrum from two to about six out of ten. None of us break the socially sacred rules of the English,[67] such as queue jumping, for example. I am not saying that we necessarily ever did, although it isn't easy to tell if you have queue jumped if the lines are Middle Eastern ones. So that is a start and gives us all one point. However, none of us say "sorry" if someone steps on our toes or bumps into us accidentally, so we will never get a full score. But then, not all of us are trying.

England can be a very tolerant place. Most Brits recognize it's OK to be different and that foreigners are bound to do things a little differently. However, there is the rub – Sam, Chloe, and Josh aren't seen as foreign, so the tolerance doesn't extend quite so far. I remember in the early days being given the most reproachful look when I had to explain pound coins, fifty pence pieces and so on to the boys as they towered above me. I am sure the shopkeeper felt that I had left this lesson a little late. Interestingly, Chloe's mid-Atlantic accent confuses people from the outset and expectations are immediately lowered in southern England if your accent is a little "odd".

Certainly, as a family we are doing much better than at the start. I very rarely have to say, "Remember English is not a swear word" any more. Nowadays we are mostly on time to appointments rather than being spectacularly early (we could never gauge how long traffic would delay us – it mostly didn't on the Cotswold lanes) or, as was more common, seriously late as we slipped into Lebanese time. On the odd occasion when all seems to be going swimmingly well, I think we really have made it, perhaps after a particularly successful dinner party when the guests appear to have enjoyed our home and family with its eclectic mix of furniture and anecdote. The impression never lasts too long, however, as my bubble will soon be burst. The last time I was so delusional I caught the entire family sitting on the lawn in the front garden, enjoying a drink.

I rushed out and asked the obvious question.

"What are you all doing?"

---

[67] Fox, *Watching the English*, p. 1.

"Having a drink in the garden," came the puzzled reply.

"Yes, I can see that, but why in the front garden? People don't sit in their front gardens!"

"It is shady in the back and sunny in the front – we want to sit in the sun," explained Susanna.

"I can see that, but have you ever seen any of our neighbours sit in their front gardens? Front gardens are to look good. You are allowed to be in them if you are gardening or walking to the front door, and that's about it. You don't sit in the front next to the roses with a glass of wine. You just can't!"

"No, what you mean is the English can't. We can!" And they continued to enjoy the wine and the sun.

Appendix

July 2014
Postscript

It is hard to believe we have been away from Lebanon for five years. I say "away" rather than "back home" because that is still how it feels, at least at a family level. Those years have been marked by epoch-changing events as the Middle East seems never out of the headlines. Even as I write, the news coming out of the region has more dramatic turns in a week than most regions experience (or at least are reported to experience) in a year. Over the last few days alone, the self-proclaimed Islamic State in Iraq and the Levant has ordered the minority Christian community in Mosul, now under its control, to convert, flee, or face a minority tax as non-Muslims or they would be killed.[68] The conflict in Gaza, now in its twelfth day, has claimed nearly 600 Palestinian and twenty-seven Israeli lives; more will die before I stop writing for the day.[69]

We had only been gone a few months when the optimistic but prematurely named Arab Spring crashed onto the world scene, following the desperate final act of Mohammed Bouazizi, the street vendor who set himself alight after his humiliation at the hands of Tunisian police. His livelihood was taken away for failing to pay the bribes and successfully navigate the state's bureaucratic maze. The nationwide outpouring of anger and explosion of repressed rage that marked the Christmas of 2010 swept away President Ben Ali in less than a month; an extraordinary end to a regime that had held power for twenty-five years. With instant communication, 24-hour

[68] www.aljazeera.com/news/middleeast/2014/07/iraq-christians-told-convert-face-death-2014718111040982432.html (accessed 6.11.14).
[69] www.theguardian.com/world/2014/jul/22/israel-gaza-israeli-soldier-missing-hamas-shujaiiya (accessed 6.11.14).

news and nightly storms on social media, the world held its breath as to where would be next. We did not have to wait long.

Just two days apart in January 2011, huge crowds came out in Cairo and Sanaa as the people of Egypt and Yemen took their anger to the streets. The targets of their wrath were the two men who had ruled their countries for more than sixty years between them. By the end of the same month, the spark of uprising caught similarly dry tinder in Sudan. It only took till mid-February and President Mubarak of Egypt had resigned. President Saleh of Yemen was harder to dislodge, but he too would be gone by November. Hardly had the Arab world time to catch its breath before it was the turn of the majority Shiites in Bahrain to demonstrate against the largely Sunni island administration. After effective government suppression, and help from the Saudi military, Bahrain dropped from the news to be replaced by a much bigger story – Libya. In the spring of 2011 the first cracks appeared in Gaddafi's iron grip on the state. The cracks gaped wide as Benghazi quickly fell to the rebels. With NATO intervention, the battles raged through the summer but with Muammar Gaddafi meeting his ignominious end in a ditch on 20 October Libya's liberation was declared.

Getting rid of a dictator is just the start of building a new and fairer society, and as Tunisia and particularly Egypt have shown, building a new social and political consensus has proved deeply difficult. If the removal of Mubarak was an earthquake, there have been many tremors since. Some have been so strong they have brought down the badly damaged social infrastructure, others were fresh earthquakes in their own right. Egypt had its first free parliamentary elections on 28 November 2011, and in June 2012 Mohamed Morsi of the Muslim Brotherhood was elected president, but by November mass protests blocked Cairo's streets once again. Lasting just over a year, Morsi's presidency came to an abrupt end when the military stepped in to depose him. With the removal of Gaddafi in Libya, groups and alliances, long suppressed, seized the world's attention as the US ambassador and three staff members were murdered when the embassy was overrun. In Tunisia, where all this started, three governments came and went in as many years and assassinations continue to rock the country.

And then, of course, there is Syria.

Taking their inspiration from the street protests of the spring of 2011, protestors came out onto the streets of Damascus and the southern city of Deraa. Initially gaining some concessions from the government, by May tanks were sent into opposition areas. Despite efforts by the Arab League and others, the situation continued to unravel until, eventually, the International Committee of the Red Cross declared what everyone had known for some time: the Syrian uprising has become a fully-fledged civil war.

Three years on and the death toll is in the region of 160,000.[70] With an estimated population in 2012 of 22.5 million people, 6.5 million are internally displaced and an estimated 2.5 million are refugees in neighbouring countries.[71] According to the UN, Syrians are about to replace Afghans as the world's largest refugee population.

The shocking news coming out of Syria and Iraq through the current summer of 2014 begged the question, was the Syrian war still just a civil war? The largely unknown acronym ISIS burst onto the world stage in June as the Sunni fighters poured out of Anbar province in Iraq to take the nation's second city of Mosul. Originally called Al-Qaeda in Iraq, it thrived in the chaos post-Saddam. Fuelled by Sunni frustrations with the sectarian nature of the Shiite-led government, the group's ambitions enlarged as they changed their name to the Islamic State of Iraq and Syria in 2013. As well as threatening the administration in Iraq, with eyes set on Baghdad, they are now major players in the Syrian conflict. Rejecting the national borders defined in the colonial period they seek to set up an Islamic caliphate in the middle of the Arab world. Today they control huge tracts of land from the eastern fringes of Aleppo in Syria to Fallujah in Iraq.

---

[70] www.nytimes.com/2014/05/20/world/middleeast/syria.html?_r=0 (accessed 6.11.14).
[71] http://syrianrefugees.eu/ (accessed 6.11.14).

The rapidly changing situation has enormous implications in the wider region. The ISIS propaganda proclaims inspiration from the Rashidun caliphate that followed the Prophet in the seventh century and attracts the disaffected from the region and further afield.[72] In Syria, however, the major opposition groups have rejected the call for such a new state. The Islamic Front have described it as devoid of legitimacy and damaging to their cause. They have been disavowed, even by Al-Qaeda, both for their military operations against other rebel fighters and their extreme acts of barbarism.

Since the maelstrom that engulfed the region post-2010 we have often been asked, did we see it coming? Along with the rest of the world, we didn't, but in many ways I wonder why we were all caught out. The ingredients were all there: autocratic governments, countless ordinary people's stories of suffering at the hands of the authorities, chronic economic underperformance, large-scale unemployment, poverty with widening inequality, rising food prices, increasing evidence of corruption among the elite classes, a malfunctioning or absent justice system with a repressive state security apparatus, the rise of political Islam fuelled by the petro dollar, and competing international agendas with Western interference in the region, to name but a few. The demonstrations that led to revolution corrected a lack of dignity that spurred individuals to action and were fuelled by the use of social media – the rapid sharing of dangerous but very different narratives to the official state propaganda.[73] Perhaps a better question is: "Why did it take so long?"

And what about Lebanon? How has it fared since 2009?

As we left, a unity government formed under the leadership of Saad Hariri. It lasted eighteen months. In June 2011 a new government formed, controlled by the Hezbollah bloc, but it lasted less than two years. From the summer of 2012, the Syrian conflict

---

[72] www.aljazeera.com/news/middleeast/2014/07/baghdadi-vision-new-caliphate-20147184858247981.html (accessed 6.11.14).

[73] www.publications.parliament.uk/pa/cm201213/cmselect/cmfaff/80/8006.htm (accessed 6.11.14).

dominated the country, with deadly clashes between Sunnis and Alawites in Tripoli and Beirut, and car and suicide bombings again rearing their ugly heads. Lebanon's sectarian make-up mirrors that of Syria, although with different proportions of the sects. Hezbollah is a natural ally of the government regime of President Assad, and the Sunni-dominated Future party is deeply sympathetic to the Syrian opposition. However, at the date of writing, Lebanon has largely managed to stay out of the conflict. That is not to say that the consequences of the conflict have stayed out of Lebanon: 1,138,043 Syrian-registered refugees are sheltering in Lebanon,[74] if you add in the unregistered, the total is 2 million,[75] making one in every three residents a refugee in an already crowded country.

These statistics hide thousands of personal stories. Wives made widows, children orphaned, and whole or remnant families displaced. When we lived in the Bekaa Valley, small encampments of tents were a seasonal affair. Agricultural workers pitched their hessian dwellings in some of the best spots by the roadside, perhaps near a clean flowing spring or in the lee of the hill. Now sprawling tent cities dominate whole areas, any flowing water is an open drain, and in winter the full force of the snowstorms rakes the thin structures with icy blasts. The Aammiq wetland reserve has had to close as the landowners seek to protect the habitats, and scientific and educational visits have been suspended. Many communities have a different feel as many thousands of strangers, their provenance and motives unknown, live up and down the valley.

Like everyone else, the A Rocha Lebanon team has been seriously affected by the regional situation. Some team members have emigrated, others have looked for more secure jobs, but the national board have been doggedly loyal and have worked against all the odds to keep the candle flame of creation care alive. With a new full-time team member, they are finding innovative ways to bring hope to a desperate situation as they work with refugees and

---

[74] http://data.unhcr.org/syrianrefugees/country.php?id=122 (accessed 6.11.14).
[75] https://www.opendemocracy.net/opensecurity/lana-asfour/lebanon-and-syrian-refugee-crisis (accessed 6.11.14).

local village communities to reforest hillsides and develop nature trails – providing paid employment for some of the most needy and an opportunity for those starved of beauty to literally "lift their eyes to the hills".[76]

---

[76] See Psalm 121:1.

The Naylor Family and the
Middle East Timeline

August 1989: Chris and Susanna arrive in Kuwait

February 1990: Chris and Susanna visit Iraq

July 1990: Chris and Susanna return to UK on holiday

August 1990: Iraqi troops invade Kuwait

January 1991: Operation Desert Storm is launched to liberate Kuwait

September 1991: Sam is born

March 1993: Chloe is born

January 1994: Chris, Susanna, Sam, and Chloe move to Amman, Jordan

October 1994: Jordan signs peace treaty with Israel, ending 46-year official
state of war

August 1995: Naylor family move to *Bayt Kassis*, Qab Elias, the Bekaa,
Lebanon

April 1996: Israeli Operation "Grapes of Wrath" targets the Bekaa and
Lebanon

January 1997: Josh is born

September 1997: Chris and Susanna start working to protect the Aammiq
wetland with A Rocha

June 1998: the Naylors move to the "lovely ugly house"

May 2000: Israel withdraws from southern Lebanon

June 2000: the Naylors move to Zahle

September 2001: 9/11 and the Naylors move to Clemenceau, Beirut

Valentine's day 2005: ex-prime minister Rafik el Hariri is assassinated

March 2005: massive pro- and anti-Syrian demonstrations grip Beirut

April 2005: Syrian forces withdraw from Lebanon

June 2005: the Naylors move to Hamra, Beirut

July to August 2006: Israel–Hezbollah war, Naylor family evacuated to Cyprus, then UK

October 2006: the Naylors return to Beirut

March 2007: the "tent city" occupation of downtown Beirut begins

May 2007: siege of the Palestinian refugee camp Nahr al-Bared following clashes between Islamist militants and the military

May 2008: at least eighty people are killed in clashes between Hezbollah and pro-government factions, sparking fears of civil war

June 2009: the Naylors relocate to UK

Suggested Reading

General Middle East

Colin Chapman, *Whose Promised Land?* Oxford: Lion, 2002.

Thomas Friedman, *From Beirut to Jerusalem*, New York, NY: Doubleday, 1989.

General Lebanon

Colin Thubron, *The Hills of Adonis*, London: Penguin, 1987. New York, NY: Vintage, 2008.

History of the Arab World

Robert Fisk, *The Great War for Civilisation: The Conquest of the Middle East*, London: Fourth Estate, 2005.

A. Hourani, *A History of the Arab Peoples*, London: Faber & Faber.

Lebanon's History

Robert Fisk, *Pity the Nation*, London: Oxford University Press, 2001.

Are Knudsen and Michael Kerr (eds) *Lebanon: After the Cedar Revolution*, London: C. Hurst & Co., 2012.

Kamal Salibi, *A House of Many Mansions*, London: I. B. Tauris, 2003.

Islam

Karen Armstrong, *Muhammad: A Biography of the Prophet*, London: Phoenix, 2001.

Suzanne Haneef, *What Everyone Should Know About Islam and Muslims*, Chicago, IL: Kazi Publications, 1979.

Tarif Khaldi, *The Qur'an: A New Translation*, London: Penguin, 2009.

A Rocha

Dave Bookless, *God Doesn't Do Waste*, Nottingham: IVP, 2010.

Dave Bookless, *Planetwise*, Nottingham: IVP, 2008.

Peter Harris, *Kingfisher's Fire*, Oxford: Monarch Books, 2008.

Peter Harris, *Under the Bright Wings*, London: Hodder & Stoughton, 1993.

Leah Kostamo, *Planted: A Story of Creation, Calling, and Community*, Oregon: Cascade Books, 2013.

LAST WORD...

If you've enjoyed this book, why not get involved with A Rocha? For more details, see www.arocha.org